HOME SMOKING AND CURING
how you can smoke-cure, salt and
preserve fish, meat and game

HOME SMOKING AND CURING

how you can smoke cure, salt and preserve fish, meat and game

KEITH ERLANDSON

BARRIE & JENKINS
COMMUNICA-EUROPA

First published in 1977 by
Barrie & Jenkins Ltd
24 Highbury Crescent London N5 1RX
Reprinted in 1978

ISBN 0 214 20322 0

Printed litho in Great Britain
by W & J Mackay Ltd, Chatham

Contents

Introduction

A few years ago, a feature appeared in one of the more responsible and less sensational Sunday newspapers, on Pinney's Smokehouse in Suffolk, which for many years had been justly famed for the production of fine smoked delicacies, notably salmon, chicken and eels. There also appeared a half-page article on smoking techniques which could be practised at home. Rudimentary salting procedures were described, together with simple smoking equipment which the average handyman could easily construct, and a few basic smoking recipes were given for food such as salmon, chicken and trout. The information was sketchy and not very accurate, but at least it did make an attempt to put the business of home smoking before the public eye. I had myself been smoke-curing for some time before this article appeared, but this was the first time I had ever seen any mention of the subject in a form which was likely to be read by a large section of the British public. The article struck me as timely, as for some years now there has been a new awareness of the pursuit of traditional crafts, such as wine- and beermaking, building furniture in one's own workshop, and curing and tanning hides and skins, to mention but a few.

In all these activities there is a considerable amount of job satisfaction, as the operator ventures into fields hitherto understood only by the masters of the various crafts.

Just as pheasant- and other game-rearing was once considered to be the province of a full-time gamekeeper, the keen
amateur has now discovered that he can rear a few dozen or
even a few hundred birds in his back garden just as efficiently
as his professional counterpart. The same applies to home
smoking.

In this age of mass production, some so-called 'smoked'
foods have no contact with real smoke but are painted with
smoke essence, which I understand is a substance similar to the
tar which collects on the interior of a smoking kiln. Good
smoked food, even when available, is very expensive. In
addition, many smoked foods are not available at all in
Britain, yet you might be very keen to try some. The answer
is to smoke them yourself. Raw products are hardly likely to
be cheap, yet even though you may pay top market price for
fresh salmon, chicken or trout, the home-smoked product will
still average out considerably cheaper than the commercially
smoked and marketed object.

Many people in Britain fish for both game and sea fish,
others shoot feathered game, and the country now has many
dedicated deer stalkers. It is to these people in particular that
a comprehensive knowledge of smoke curing can be so useful.
In particular it offers alternative ways of eating their catches
of fish and bags of game. A surfeit of fresh salmon palls and
there are surely limits to the amount of roast or casseroled
game and wildfowl a person would wish to eat.

The commercial smoker must cater for the 'average palate',
but we all know full well that, in reality, no such thing as the
average palate exists, particularly in the matter of salt or
other seasoning. As a home-smoker, you are in a position to
have your product salty or mild, lightly or heavily smoked.
You can experiment and vary the process until you find one
exactly to your liking; so, through no fault of the commercial
smoker, the home smoker should be able to produce a far
more satisfactory product, to his or her own taste, than could
be bought in the shops.

There is still a great dearth of reliable information on home
smoking. Librarians are apt to look askance when you ask if
they have any books on the subject, and the only one I have
come across, although excellent, does not go into any great

detail when describing some processes.

However, I am particularly indebted to the staff of the Torry Research Station, Aberdeen and the Food and Agricultural Organization of the United Nations, who have published pamphlets on the smoke curing of fish and the construction of smoke houses. I must stress the need for experimentation and the working out of suitable techniques by trial and error, and freely admit that a skilled operator, using simple traditional equipment, can produce better results than an unskilled or careless person operating a sophisticated mechanical smoker costing many thousands of pounds.

Working on the broad principles of fish smoking, I have evolved my own methods and equipment for the smoking of poultry, meat and game, by the trial and error method and with (ultimate) complete success. I hope to be able to instruct my readers in the next few chapters to prepare most of the smoked delicacies enjoyed at the moment in other European countries, and others which I believe at the present time are exclusive in this country to me.

1

The origins of smoke curing

It is impossible to define the precise point in the history of mankind when the smoke curing of fish and meat came into being. Possibly it was discovered during the Stone Age, when primitive man used fires to warm himself and cook his food, having fish or meat hanging in the same cave or shelter as the fire. He may have discovered that the food acquired a distinctive and pleasant flavour through being brought into contact with wood smoke, and that the keeping qualities were considerably enhanced — a most important consideration, as he depended on hunting. There might be times when he and his companions would succeed in driving a whole herd of reindeer into a roughly constructed enclosure and a great killing would take place. A mammoth might be taken in a game pit, or a fresh run of salmon could supply them with a great quantity of fish. In all these cases the hunters would have far more food than would be required for their immediate needs, but these early forbears of ours were sufficiently intelligent and far-sighted to realize that some time hence, game might be temporarily scarce or non-existent, and the salmon run always came to an end eventually. It is therefore perfectly logical to suppose that primitive man had a keen interest in preserving his surplus food against leaner times, when a supply of smoked or dried fish or flesh could spell the difference between survival and oblivion.

Again, it is impossible to define when pre-salting or brining was adopted as an essential part of the process as it is recognized today. It is safe to say that, the higher the salt content in a product and the longer the smoking period employed, the better its keeping qualities will be.

About forty miles from where I write, on the tidal reaches of Conway, is an ancient stone-built salmon trap. Within a few yards of this trap is a cave, whose mouth is covered at high tide. The interior of the cave rises upwards, above the water level, and according to local legend the Romans used to smoke their salmon in this cave, probably lighting their fire at low tide. The cave mouth would have been sealed by the rising tide, and the salmon were ready by the time the tide receded again.

I think we can safely dismiss the story of the first finnan haddock. It is said that a Scottish fisherman by the name of Finson customarily hung his haddock catches to dry by his barn. One night the barn caught fire, though most of the catch was ruined, Finson managed to salvage a few of the less damaged ones. These were eaten and enjoyed, and so finnan haddock came into being. To me, this sounds impossible. Intense heat would be generated by the burning barn, sufficient to cook the fish, even though it would be sufficiently out of reach to escape being burned to a cinder. Finnan haddock requires a very gentle smoking process, not in excess of 85° F, otherwise it will cook and disintegrate.

2

Smoked fish and game in Scandinavia

A few years ago my wife and I did an extensive tour of the Scandinavian peninsular, covering a distance of over 4,000 miles. Apart from the cleanliness and very obvious prosperity of the two countries visited (Norway and Sweden), I was particularly impressed by the manner in which the Scandinavians utilize their natural resources of fish and game.

Upon landing in Bergen, my first call was to a fishmonger. Memories thirty-six years old of smoked mackerel still lingered, and we secured a supply. When we ate them the following day on the way to Trondheim, we found them oily-skinned and difficult to dismember — very palatable, but not as memory told me they should be. A visit to Trondheim fish market was an education and cleared up the doubts about the mackerel. Everything seemed larger than life. Huge salmon, fresh and smoked, reposed upon the slabs. The lobsters varied from ordinary to the gigantic and the halibut were the largest I have seen. Sea bream were much in evidence, split open and rather glutinous in appearance and there were mackerel, fresh and smoked. There were two types of smoked mackerel, the dark, oily kind we had already sampled and others with wrinkled golden skins, which I then realised were the excellent hot smoked variety, ready to eat, which we wanted. We realized then that the Bergen mackerel were only cold smoked and needed cooking. We had eaten them raw.

In a Lapland supermarket we purchased fresh grayling and smoked perch. The perch are very highly esteemed in Sweden and are the same price as smoked trout. When I considered the many thousands of perch which must be returned to water annually by coarse fishermen in Britain, I realized we were missing something. My wife and son did not care for the perch but I found them excellent and quite unique. They were dark, firm and waxy fleshed with a powerful flavour.

At Jokkmok, a former Lapp village, now a small but important town, we purchased some lightly smoked reindeer haunch, which, owing to the mackerel experience, we realized we would have to cook. We fried it at the roadside and found it quite palatable, although we felt we could have improved upon it with more time, knowledge and additives.

Further south, a visit to Stockholm game market proved well worthwhile. The stalls were decorated with elk heads and stuffed goshawks, and, although the game season had not started, there were several specimens from cold store, including a fair quantity of ptarmigan in full winter plumage, all with their feet removed (grouse claw brooches?). These were accompanied by a rather weary-looking hen capercaillie and three even more unappetising mallard, priced at £1.55 each. Even more surprisingly priced were oven-ready wood pigeon at 70p each. I was asked £8.50 for a haunch of smoked roe but settled for a kilo. This was hot smoked and ready to eat, and was quite delicious. We also saw smoked badger hams, pike, huge smoked eels and masses of freshwater crayfish.

Back in my own province of Bohuslan, on the west coast, we looked up the daughter of a famous local hunter, whom I knew thirty-six years previously. His main quarry were roe, elk and willow grouse, which he shot over an English setter. This lady was able to fill me in on how an elk is dealt with. A young elk will provide excellent steaks, but what, I asked, does one do with an old bull as big as a Shire horse? They are best made into meat balls. Being dry fleshed, it is better to mix them with pork in equal quantities. I do know that BB shot works out at 70 pellets to the ounce. How many meat balls to an elk?

While on the west coast we took a day trip to Oslo, mainly to see the Viking ships. However, I found a fishmonger offering the only cheap food of the whole tour, grayling at 27½p per pound. They were large fish running three to a kilo, and my wife cooked them using a trout recipe. Nothing could have been better. They were entirely different in character from a Welsh grayling, they were deeper and fatter, more silvery and with tiny mouths. In flavour they were the equal of any salmon. Our local ones taste like the bed of the Dee.

We found so many good things to eat on our trip, particularly of the smoked variety, which are either completely unobtainable in this country or can only be found at considerable trouble and expense, that we decided to develop our own smoking techniques, using simple traditional methods as practised by the Lapps, Red Indians and the small Scottish salmon curers.

3

The basic smoking process

I think at this point we might consider exactly what modern smoking processes consist of.

Salting

Before smoking commences, the raw materials are either dry salted or soaked in brine. As previously stated, the salt content helps to preserve the product, but this is now less important. Owing to modern storage and refrigeration techniques, it is not so much to preserve food that smoking is employed in the western hemisphere, but to give it a pleasant and distinctive flavour, the salt acting more as a seasoning than a preservative. These remarks do not, however, apply to hot countries like Africa and the Far East, where the preservation of the catch is of the utmost importance.

Humidity and weight loss

During the actual smoking process, tarry deposits from the smoke settle on the product. These deposits are of an antiseptic nature and, along with the salt already absorbed, tend to inhibit the development of the spoilage bacteria, which, left to their own devices, cause fish or flesh to putrify. During smoking, weight loss occurs in the product, due to evaporation of moisture from within the tissues. Indeed this evaporation and subsequent weight loss are absolutely essential to successful smoking, and it follows that the greater the weight loss, the greater the keeping qualities. This weight loss is directly linked to the humidity of the atmosphere prevailing at the time of smoking, so that in a traditional kiln a side of salmon or a fillet of beef will take longer to dry out sufficiently under humid conditions than under relatively dry ones. In the modern mechanical kiln, humidity is controlled automatically, so these variations in smoking times do not occur, but the home smoker using traditional methods must always be aware of this factor and be prepared to allow for it accordingly.

There are two methods of smoking employed in European countries — hot and cold smoking.

Cold smoking

Cold smoking smokes but does not cook the product. It is usually done at temperatures between 50 and 85°F, ideally, 75 - 80° F. Cold smoking temperatures are, to a certain extent, governed by outside temperatures. Where ambient temperatures are low, it is quite possible to smoke successfully at far lower temperatures than available literature suggests is possible, provided one is prepared to spend more time on the process. At a time of high ambient temperatures, it is important that smoking temperatures are kept sufficiently low in the case of fish, or the product will cook and disintegrate. Some cold smoked products are eaten raw, e.g. salmon, cod roes and beef fillets, whereas others, such as finnan haddock, kippers and cod fillets, require a further period of cooking in the kitchen.

Hot smoking

Hot smoked products, after salting or brining, are first cold smoked for varying periods to dry them out partially and to impart a smoked flavour. In the case of fish, the temperature is then raised to about 180° F — never more than 200° F — and the fish are cooked for a time in the hot smoke. Care must be taken during the initial cold smoking that temperatures do not exceed 85° F or the fish will case harden, preventing further smoke penetration or adequate loss of moisture.

Meat, poultry and game are easier to hot smoke than fish, although much less is known about their processing. Care must be exercised during their cold smoking periods to avoid case hardening, as in the case of fish, and for exactly the same reasons. However during their hot smoking periods these meats are far more tolerant of variations in temperature, and a range of 180 - 240° F might be suitable for the same product, though a batch of fish would be ruined in the higher temperature ranges. Nevertheless, even these relatively tolerant products can be spoilt by excessive temperatures or overcooking. Apart from becoming unacceptably dry in texture, the product tends to lose its smoky character, so an overdone haunch of venison will simply resemble dry roast meat.

Once the basic principles are mastered and, in particular, the correct salt content, it is surprising just how cheap and easy it is to manufacture really first-class smoked products.

4

The raw material

Fish

There is a completely erroneous belief in some quarters that stale fish can be used for smoking, as the smoking process will impart its own flavour to the fish and thus mask any defects in quality. Certainly it is just possible to 'save the life' of stale fish approaching putrefaction, by smoking, so that it is just edible; but, at the best, only a very inferior product both in keeping quality and flavour can result.

Fish which is to be smoked *must* be completely fresh to obtain the best results, although this is a good point at which to dispel the belief that frozen goods are not suitable for smoking. This is completely untrue. All deep frozen fish, game, meat and poultry can be employed, and first-class results obtained.

However, in the case of salmon, a better-looking finished product can be obtained from fresh fish. This is because the moisture between the fibres of course turns to ice within the fish during deep freezing. When the fish is allowed to thaw out, prior to smoking, this water runs away, taking some of the fish's natural oil with it; however carefully the fish is filleted, some gaps will appear between the fibres of the cut surface, causing a more unsightly finish than if the cut surface could be kept smooth and unblemished. Deep frozen salmon is altogether more tender to handle when thawed out than the fresh fish.

Fat content

This mention of the oil loss suffered by the thawed-out salmon, brings one to the connection between the relative fat contents of all raw products to be smoked and the salt contents they are required to absorb during pre-salting or brining. Anything with a high fat content is more resistent to salt penetration than anything with a lower concentration of fat. It follows, therefore, that a fat, fresh run salmon will require longer in the brine than a fish of equal size that has been hanging about a river during a period of low water, or alternatively, has come many miles inland, negotiating scores of obstacles on the way. I was told a story of a Scottish salmon smoker who attended to the needs of several fishermen who fished the length of a famous salmon river. At one period when he was extremely busy and his kiln was full to capacity, a friend called in and was shown fish from practically every beat on the river. Even to an unpractised eye, it was apparent that the best conditioned fish came from the lower reaches of the river, and the higher up the river the fish had been caught, the thinner they became.

There are no hard and fast rules to apply to this question of differing fat content. One must play it by ear and use intelligent guesswork. If I am brining a batch of pheasants and I notice one is lacking in fat under the skin, it comes out of the brine 15 minutes before the others; if I am preparing fillets of beef and some have that marbling of fat between the tissues, visible at the sliced ends and the hallmark of superbly conditioned cattle, they receive 30 minutes longer in the brine than the very lean, solid red fillets.

Meat

Whereas fish for smoking should be as fresh as possible, which should present no problem to the home smoker, who will in the majority of cases be a fisherman himself and smoke his own fresh catches, other products require a different approach. Beef will not absorb salt unless it has been hanging for a minimum of one week, and 10 days to a fortnight is better here. It is essential to know and trust one's butcher. So many modern butchers do not hang their meat for long enough before selling, but there are still some old-fashioned rural butchers who do. Ideally, the beef should hang in the carcase, but if only fresh fillets can be obtained they can be 'aged' in a refrigerator (not a deep freeze). They will probably become a little tainted when ageing in a refrigerator, but a wash in vinegar solution before brining will take care of this problem. No meat or game should be allowed to become really high before smoking as a gamey taste conflicts with the smoky flavour, and I find it unpleasant. Venison should hang for one week to 10 days. Pheasants, grouse, mallard, ducks, geese, turkeys and chickens are best done fairly fresh, 3 days dead being ideal. I have smoked thousands of quail which have been deep frozen within 24 hours of killing, and this would appear to be perfectly satisfactory.

Deep freeze storage

In the deep freeze storage of any foods required for smoking, all ageing must be done when the product is in its fresh condition, and it must be processed immediately upon thawing out. Salmon should be stored with their heads on and guts intact. As they do not feed in fresh water, their innards are empty, so gut tainting does not result. Trout should be gutted and the blood channel along the spine scraped out before freezing. Eel guts taint very rapidly, so they should be gutted as soon as possible, but the chief secret of successful eel smoking is the removal of the kidney. The eel has one kidney, buried deep in the flesh — 1½ in. *below* the vent. You must slice into this area and scrape out the kidney, for if it is left within the eel it will make the finished product unpalatable.

All poultry and winged game should be plucked and drawn prior to deep freezing. I once froze a batch of pheasants intact but they suffered a certain degree of gut tainting. Although still quite palatable, knowing their history as I did, I could just detect a degree of tainting although others did not.

If you intend to store anything in the deep freeze for any length of time, it is an excellent idea to wrap it in either aluminium foil or brown paper, which will protect it from freezer burn and subsequent dehydration to a far greater degree than polythene freezer bags.

5

Pre-salting

As I have already mentioned, the addition of salt to the raw
material is an essential part of the smoke curing process. The
product is either completely covered in dry salt for a period,
or soaked in brine of varying strengths according to what is
being processed.

Dry salting is favoured by the commercial fish smoking
concerns, particularly in the case of salmon, as the dry salt
attracts moisture from the tissues of the fish, causing a weight
loss of up to 9% during this part of the process. It follows,
therefore, that the time the fish will need in the smoking
kiln will be much reduced, as about half the weight loss
required in the finished product will already have taken place.
So the whole process can be speeded up, and of course in any
commercial enterprise time means money. To home smokers,
speeding the process is not important, as in any case they will
be conducting the operation partly as a hobby. I have no
hesitation, therefore, in recommending the use of brine as
opposed to dry salt (but see 'Dry Salting and other methods',
below).

Brining

In common with all minority activities of a traditional nature,
there are a number of closely guarded 'secrets' connected with

smoke curing. So it is with smoke curing. In bygone days, other secret ingredients were added to the brines: brown sugar, molasses, rum, white pepper, salpetre, cloves and bay leaves, all of which were alleged to impart additional flavour to smoked salmon; yet all that is required to make a first-class smoked product is pure vacuum-dried salt, which is very cheap.

Originally, wooden brining tubs were employed. Metal is to be avoided as it can taint the product. Modern plastic vessels are particularly suitable, and a plastic dustbin is ideal. Crockery or earthenware vessels can also be used for brining small quantities of food.

As the home smoker is unlikely to be dealing with large quantities of food at any one time, there is no reason why you should not use a fresh lot of brine for everything you process. This is far more hygenic than keeping used brine and adding more salt to it in order to keep the strength up to the required level, as bacteria can breed in stale brine.

In large smoking plants it is customary to use the same lot of brine for several batches of fish, adding more salt and checking the concentration of the brine by floating a salino-meter in the liquid. This instrument gives a reading of the salt concentration. The raw product absorbs salt from the brine solution, causing it to become weaker, hence the need to add more solid salt. The most widely used brine is an 80% solution, which is formed by dissolving 2 lb 10¾ oz of salt in each gallon of water. Make the solution by adding the salt to 3 pints of hot or boiling water, giving it a good stir to dissolce the salt partly, then adding another 5 pints of cold water and stirring again. As some products require different brine strengths, a table is given in Appendix 2.

When brining, it is not a good idea to pack the fish or other articles too closely together, otherwise the brine may be denied access to all parts. As they will float to the surface, they must be weighted down, so that they remain at all times completely submerged. A good idea is to place a wire cake cooling rack on the surface, with a fairly heavy object such as a 7-lb weight on top of the rack. A ½-gallon plastic ice cream box partially filled with water also makes a convenient weight. During the brining period, it is advisable to lift the weight once or twice and agitate the contents. After the brine has been used, it can be re-used as a good non-selective weed-killer, particularly on waste ground or garden paths. Brining tubs should always be well washed after use.

Fish should always be brined separately from meat, poultry or game, or these other products will become fish-tainted. There is, however, no objection to their sharing the same smoking kiln later on.

Strong and weak brines

My own preference is for a fairly strong brine (80 - 90%) in which the fish, fowl or flesh is left for a matter of hours rather than days, but there is an alternative method, involving the use of weaker brines, plus sugar and in some cases other ingredients. The material is left in these weaker brines often for a period of several days, and though it is not usual to brine fish in this manner, the method has a definite place in the curing of certain meats and fowl which, owing to their age or species, are likely to be very tough.

Salt has a hardening effect upon the muscular tissue of mammalian and avian flesh, but sugar tenderizes, so a tough bird such an aged goose, pheasant or turkey could benefit from treatment in sugar-added brine. However, where the method really comes into its own is when you have to deal with a piece of less than prime quality beef or a joint of elderly bear, elk or wild boar. The British home smoker is hardly likely to be faced with any of these last three commodities. Even if you have friends in the USA or Scandinavia who might conceivably send you some of these meats, the Ministry of Agriculture would hardly be kindly disposed to their importation. Nevertheless the method could prove very useful in brining of venison from an old stag, and it is also customary to use this so-called 'sweet pickle' brining method when curing bacon or ham, either smoked or unsmoked. When strong brines are employed for a few hours, the temperature of the brine is of little consequence as the food does not remain in the pickle for any length of time, but when using the longer 'sweet pickle' brining process certain procedures must be observed. When a lengthy brining process is involved, the pickle should first be chilled to about 35° F before the meat is immersed. Throughout the entire length of the cure, the liquid must be maintained at this temperature by refrigeration to prevent spoilage. However, if you notice that the brine is beginning to smell sour, pour it away at once and wash the meat in a weak vinegar solution. The vessel should be washed out and scalded and a fresh batch of pickle made.

Whether you use the short, strong brining process or the longer one involving sweet pickle, the contents of the brining vessel should be agitated from time to time. Brine weakens towards the surface, so the agitation will ensure that the brine remains at a more consistent strength; when brining in sweet pickle for several days, it is a good idea to turn the meat or birds over daily.

Sweet pickle

    8½ gallons water
    5 lbs vacuum-dried salt
    1 lb white sugar
    1 oz saltpetre
    4 oz pickling spice

Brine for octopus or squid

    6½ gallons water
    10½ oz salt
    2 lb brown sugar
    62 fl. oz soy sauce
    3 cups lemon juice
    4 tablespoons garlic juice
    4 tablespoons onion juice
    6 tablespoons ground ginger

Vacuum-dried salt can be purchased from most agricultural merchants, and if you scan the yellow pages of your telephone directory an entry under 'salt merchants' will usually be discovered. Salt attracts atmospheric moisture, so it is worth paying a few more pence for salt packed in a stout plastic sack than a paper one. It is best stored in a closed container such as a plastic domestic dustbin with a well-fitting lid. If salt does become damp and lumpy it will still be fit to use, but bulk for bulk will weigh a little heavier than dry salt owing to the moisture it has absorbed; if using damp salt, 2 - 3 oz more per gallon of water should be used than recommended in the tables.

The brining pump

Brine has a very penetrative effect upon the tissues of fish and flesh. The salt content of the brine blends with the fluid content of the meat or fish and works its way through the tissues towards the interior. However, when very thick pieces of meat or very large birds are being processed, there may be such a depth of flesh that it is difficult for the brine to penetrate right to the interior. An aid to effective penetration is the brine pump, which works on exactly the same principle as the hypodermic syringe, except that the brine is forced out of holes in the side of the needle instead of the tip.

The greatest advantage of the brining pump is that it can be plunged in close to the bone of hams and large haunches of venison, as it is around the bones where a type of deterioration called 'bone tainting' can arise.

If the pump has been out of action for some time, the plunger should be soaked in water for 3 hours to soften and expand it. Before filling, the needle should be sterlizied by holding it under boiling water for 20 seconds. The needle should be dipped into the brine until its entire length is covered, then the plunger should be fully withdrawn and the cylinder of the syringe is filled. The needle should be driven into the flesh at an angle, right to the bone, but the full charge of brine should not be deposited at this point. As the plunger is depressed, the needle should be slowly drawn out and will distribute brine around its path to the surface. When the needle is withdrawn, the tissues around the exit hole should be firmly pressed with the fingers to prevent the brine leaking out.

It is most important that the pump should be kept scrupulously clean, otherwise bacteria as well as brine may be injected into the meat. About 1 fl. oz per 1 lb of meat should be injected. The meat should then be immersed in brine for

Brine pump

the usual period, to ensure maximum distribution of brine throughout the tissues. The brine pump should be used as a piece of auxiliary equipment, not as an end in itself. After use, the pump should be dismantled, then thoroughly washed and dried before it is put away.

Dry salting and other methods

In addition to the strong brines which I favour for use in most of my own smoking and curing operations, and the sweet pickle brine already described for use during other processes, I will also outline alternative brining methods and seasoning techniques, and dry salting methods for fish curing which you may prefer since dry salting removes more water from the fish during the curing process than does brining. The smoking process can then be appreciably shortened, as the fish only needs to make half the total required weight loss during actual smoking as the other half has already been lost during dry salting.

To dry salt fish, either filleted or split, a bed of either plain vacuum-dried salt, or special dry cure, which I will describe later, should be made about 1 in. thick on a wooden or plastic surface. When several fish are to be dry salted, a stack of fish should be formed by laying a split fish, or two fillets side by side, skin side down on the bed of salt. The cut surfaces should be covered with a ½-in. layer of salt over the thickest parts of the fish, thinning to a mere sprinkling towards the thinnest parts of the tails. Another split fish or pair of fillets is then placed on top of this layer of salt, skin side down, and the process repeated until the stack is complete, the last layer of fish being covered with a ½-in. layer of salt or special cure (see below), with the exception of the tail. The salting time varies according to size, fat content and species of fish involved. Small salmon fillets (1½ - 2 lb) require about 5 - 6 hours. Medium fillets (3 - 4 lb) require 8 - 9 hours, while fillets of 5 lb and upwards will require 12 - 14 hours. Note that, in the case of split fish, double the weight of a certain sized fillet only requires salting for the same length of time as quoted for a single fillet. During the salting process brine will be formed as water is extracted from the fish and drains away from the stack of fish. After salting, the fish should be well washed in cold water to remove all traces of surface salt, then soaked in fresh water for 5 minutes and hung up to dry for 24 hours. In the case of non-fatty fish such as cod or haddock, salting times should be decreased by 25%.

Dry cure for fish

- 8 lb salt
- 4 lb brown sugar
- 2 oz saltpetre
- 4 tablespoons white pepper
- 2 tablespoons garlic powder

Special dry cure for fish

- 8 lb salt
- 4 lb brown sugar
- 2 oz saltpetre
- 6 tablespoons garlic powder
- 6 tablespoons crushed cloves
- 6 tablespoons onion powder
- 6 tablespoons crushed bay leaves
- 6 tablespoons crushed mace

Pre-drying

With the exception of trout and eels, which are placed in the smoker when wet with brine, most products will benefit by a pre-drying period before being placed in the smoker. This will get rid of any excess moisture and will reduce the smoking period required accordingly. It is recommended that salmon sides should hang in a room at about 70° F for 24 hours prior to smoking, or at least overnight. Poultry, venison, game and beef should hang for the same period, but small birds such as quail, grouse and woodcock only need to pre-dry for about 3 hours. Of course the relative humidity of the atmosphere will have some bearing on the required pre-drying period, so one must again 'play it by ear'. It is rather important that small birds, pheasants, venison, beef and fish should be protected from a drying wind when pre-drying, otherwise they will case harden, with the same results as if over-rapid smoke drying was allowed to take place (domestic ducks would not be similarly affected, owing to the very oily nature of their skins).

6

Fuels

Wood for smoke production

The essential commodity upon which the success of any smoke curing operation depends is a suitable supply of smoke-producing fuel. What is required is a fuel which will burn slowly and steadily, requiring the minimum of attention, and without producing too much heat. Non-resinous woods must be used as resinous soft woods impart a bitter flavour to the food, although giving it an attractive colour. Some people mix a proportion of softwood sawdust with that of the hardwood variety, which they claim adds colour without impairing the flavour of the smoked product.

Basically, any British hardwood can be used for smoke production. Oak is traditional but beech, ash, elm, sycamore and hickory are all perfectly suitable, or any mixture of these. The Lapps use birch almost exclusively, with, I suspect, some alder. Spanish oak must be avoided as it gives the food a rather unpleasant antiseptic flavour. Sawdust, chips, or small logs of all these woods can be used, but if fires of solid fuel are made, they will require regular attention. At times they will flare up and cook the product, if not restrained. At other times they will die down and need replenishing. The most consistent fuel of all is sawdust. It does not flare into life but smoulders with a steady glow for hours on end, producing a fairly consistent column of smoke; 1½ - 2 biscuit-tinfuls of oak sawdust will, if placed in a suitable receptacle, burn without attention for 12 - 15 hours. Having stated that sawdust is my preference, I will add that branches of juniper or gorse can be added to the final stages of salmon smoking; they are aromatic but non-resinous woods, and can add a distinctive flavour to the salmon.

Sources of supply

There now arises the essential question of the source of supply of the fuel of your choice. At most sawmills, the sawdust from all operations goes into a large collective sump. In addition to the essential British hardwoods, the sump will in all probability contain sawdust of pine, larch and spruce, in addition to those of foreign timbers such as mahogany, teak and iroku. This conglomerate mixture is quite unsuitable for smoking. Look for small, rural sawmills, particularly in stock-raising areas where there is a steady demand for hardwood stock-fencing stakes. These stakes are trimmed and pointed individually at a sawbench; consequently the sawdust from them is unadulterated by unsuitable timbers, and a few sackfuls can usually be reserved for the smoker by a co-operative foreman.

Hot smoking fuels

In addition to his smoke-producing fuel, the smoker will also require a fuel to produce sufficient heat for hot smoking various products. Although small logs will provide sufficient heat, these fires are difficult to control to the correct temperatures, so in all my own hot smoking operations I use Calor gas and gas rings. How, I will explain later. I see no reason why electrical elements should not be incorporated in a hot smoker by any handyman competent in these matters, but being one of those persons with such a horror of electricity that I don rubber boots and gloves to change a torch battery, I will leave such ventures to those more knowledgeable.

In addition to the hardwoods already mentioned, hedgerow woods such as hawthorn and blackthorn can be used. Apple, pear, plum and damson are all excellent, and have the added advantage of imparting a particularly pleasant flavour to the product. However, as these woods are not sawn commercially but are normally used as fuel only in rural areas, it will hardly be possible to obtain them in the convenient form of sawdust or chips. Thinly cut slices of these woods can, however, be cut with a chain saw, and large logs from mature fruit trees can be split with an axe to produce conveniently sized and readily combustible pieces. To prevent these solid fuels from bursting into flame and producing excessive heat, the wood should be kept damp, but a disadvantage of this practice is that damp fuel produces smoke which is heavily moisture-laden. The product receiving attention will there take far longer to dry out under these circumstances, consequently prolonging the process. This situation can be avoided by damping down with dry sand the fire burning solid fuel.

At one time, a salmon smoker pursued his craft in a particularly treeless area in the west of Ireland, where the supply of fresh salmon was excellent but the supply of fuel was restricted to peat. On being asked how he managed to find a supply of suitable smoke-producing fuel in such a timberless land, this worthy gentleman revealed that he had a working arrangement with the local undertaker who imported oak and other hardwood boards for the manufacture of coffins, so was able to keep the salmon smoker supplied with wood chips and offcuts, all dry and nicely seasoned.

Another acquaintance of mine lived in South Africa for a time and was fond of smoking mackerel and snoek, which he caught in considerable numbers off Capetown. His smoking kiln consisted of a derelict upright-type refrigerator with part of the top cut away. His fuel was obtained from the local brewery, which apparently manufactured its own oak barrels and was able to supply my friend with chips, shavings and offcuts in the same manner that the undertaker supplied the Irishman. So if you find difficulty at first in finding suitable fuels, you would be well advised to consider whether there are any local industries in your particular district which might be able to keep you supplied.

7

Equipment

The traditional cold smoker

Cold smoking, at temperatures of around 80° F, is an essential operation for the production of smoked salmon, which is eaten raw, of other smoked fish, such as kippers, finnan haddocks, cod and haddock fillets and cod roes, and fillets of beef. Cold smoking is also an essential part of the initial processing of all other products which are ultimately hot smoked.

In the commercial fish smoking industry, the traditional cold smoking kiln is simply a large chimney with ventilators placed up the shaft at intervals, so that draughts can be controlled. The fire is lit in a large hearth either at the foot of the kiln or in a fire pit a few feet away, the smoke being conducted along an underground flue to the kiln by natural draught. At intervals, the positions of the various racks of fish undergoing treatment have to be changed around, so that all the fish receive even smoke treatment. The task of going up a smoke-filled flue is an unpleasant one, so small wonder that the fish-smoking industry is turning to mechanical kilns, where the smoke can be shut off while the fish trolleys are rearranged.

It is a fairly simple matter for the home smoker to construct a kiln on the traditional principle which is simpler in design

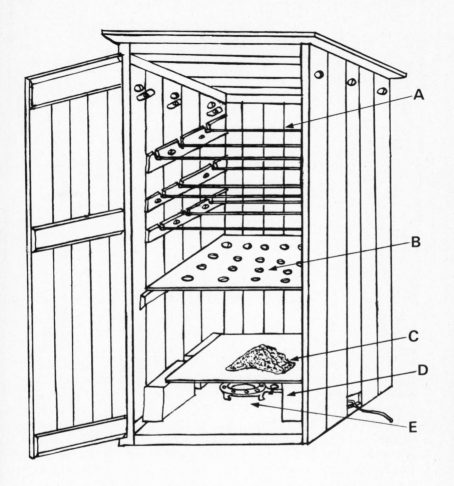

A Support rods
B Smoke spreader
C Metal plate for fuel
D Brick supports
E Gasring

Wooden cold smoker

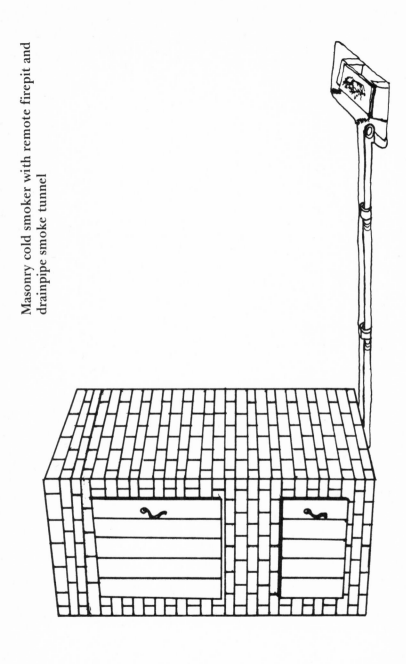

Masonry cold smoker with remote firepit and drainpipe smoke tunnel

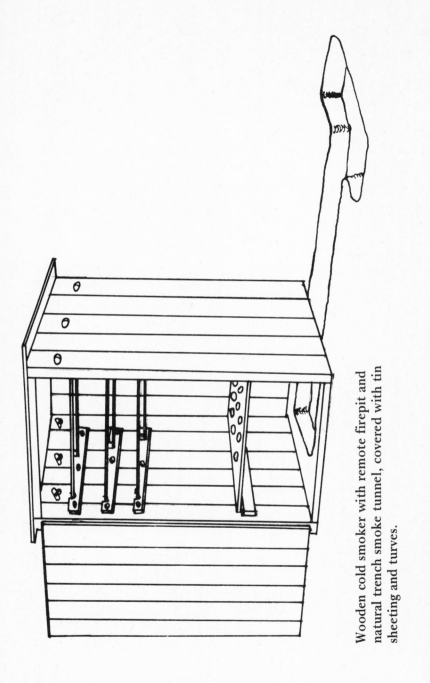

Wooden cold smoker with remote firepit and natural trench smoke tunnel, covered with tin sheeting and turves.

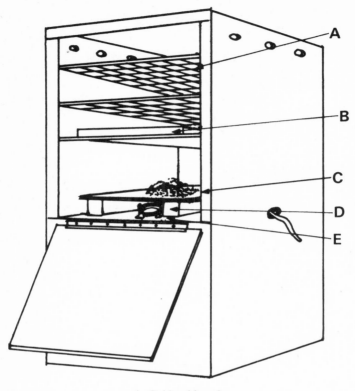

A Gridweld racks
B Dripping tin
C Metal plate for fuel
D Supporting bricks
E Gasring

Oil cabinet smoker

and which is sufficient for his needs. For home use, a kiln 6 or 7 ft high and 2 - 3 ft in width and depth, with a wide open hearth at the bottom, will be adequate, or the principle of the remote fire pit and underground flue can be employed. The kiln may be constructed of stone, brick or, more economically still, concrete blocks, or even wood providing the fire pit is not too close. Tin sheeting should be avoided as metal is too quickly affected by temperature, and a metal cold smoker

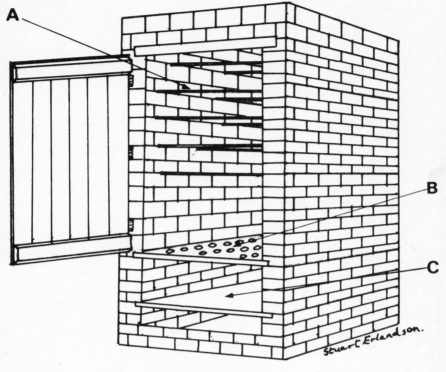

A *Built-in support rods*
B *Smoke spreader*
C *Plate for holding fuel*

Masonry cold smoker

will soon become a hot smoker when a strong sun shines upon it. The kiln should have a close-fitting door with vent holes 1 - 2 in. below the roof, and preferably a perforated plate below the actual smoking chamber to assist an even smoke spread. It should if at all possible stand in a sheltered spot to avoid excessive draughts. An old, disused (of course!) stone or brick outside toilet can be converted into an excellent smoke house and this likeness is often commented on. A Welsh friend, speaking of a smoking kiln at a local estate owners' residence, described it as, 'Like a *Ty Bach*' (small

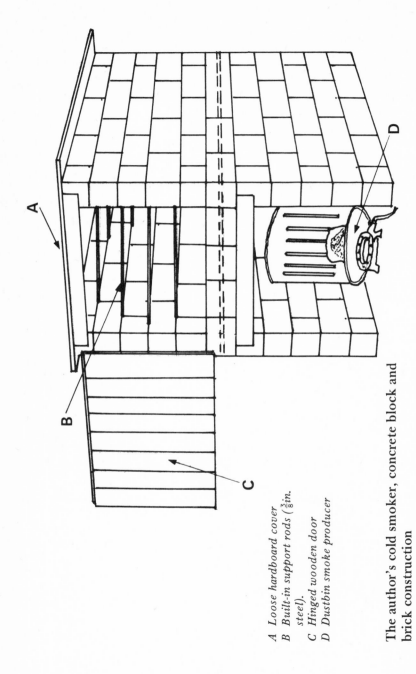

A Loose hardboard cover
B Built-in support rods ($\frac{3}{8}in.$ steel).
C Hinged wooden door
D Dustbin smoke producer

The author's cold smoker, concrete block and brick construction

house), and a newspaper reporter, doing a review on Pinney's famous smokehouse in Suffolk, described the kilns as being, 'Small, like two smoke blackened privies'.

The interior must be fitted with some means of suspending the articles to be smoked, either rods supplied with hooks or fittings to accommodate sliding trays.

A thermometer, with one or two spares in case of breakages, will be required, and it is a good idea to buy the kind which will register up to 240° F, so that they may also be used for hot smoking. This can pose something of a problem as most household thermometers will only register up to about 120° F. I am told a jam thermometer is ideal but they are expensive and not always easy to find, and a mechanical kiln thermometer is very expensive indeed. I managed to solve this problem by finding a firm which sells laboratory supplies.

So that my own kiln should not be too affected by fluctuating temperatures, I built it inside an old disused dairy with 15-in. stone walls, which keeps cool in summer. I would make an infinitely better ballerina than bricklayer, so the building of the kiln was a monumental task. I used concrete blocks and some old bricks I had lying around, made a wooden door frame for the smoking chamber, and tailored an old stable half-door almost to fit the frame. I built against the dairy wall, thereby saving the effort of building a fourth side, and such were the irregularities along the top of its three walls, brought about through my inexpertise, that the simple addition of a sheet of loose hardboard provided a roof with adequate ventilation. Nevertheless, it is entirely functional and, unlike a mechanical kiln, is so foolproof and reliable that even I cannot cause it to go wrong.

The building of it is one of my proudest achievements and when a Swedish friend visited me from the gundog world, a sphere in which I have earned a little more acclaim than my building exploits are ever likely to produce, I was able to inform him proudly, 'This is the *Rökhus*.'

My kiln has a large, open hearth, but to place a pile of sawdust in it is somewhat wasteful, as more seems to be consumed than is necessary for smoke production. I burnt my sawdust in a galvanized dustbin which can be slid in and out of the hearth. There is a 6-in. hole cut in the side near the bottom of the bin to allow the draught to enter, and to start my fire I tilt the bin and ignite one of my Calor gas rings under the metal of the dustbin floor, which I perforated with a cold chisel.

The two biscuit-tinfuls of sawdust in the bin burn for many hours, and the system of replenishment is similar to that of the chain smoker who lights a new cigarette from the butt of the last. I rake the ash out of the hole with a small shovel, then move the remaining sawdust, which is smouldering at the back of the bin, forward to the hole. I put another tinful of fresh sawdust in behind the old stuff, which quickly ignites the new, then I can go to bed if I so desire, secure in the knowledge that, while I am sleeping, my kiln is working.

Hot smoking kilns

Pressure smoking

The first piece of smoking equipment I had any experience with was the Abu Smokebox, which is manufactured by Abu Svangsta of Sweden, a famous firm of fishing tackle manufacturers. The Abu measures about 12 x 7 x 4 in. deep and on account of its small size, the potential is very limited. The Abu works on a different principle from other smoke units, and is said to 'pressure smoke'. A bed of fine sawdust is spread on its floor, and a combined drip tin and wire rack placed over the sawdust, on which is placed the food to be smoked. A small methylated spirit burner under the Abu supplies instant heat, and the sliding lid fits fairly tightly into place. Here the process differs from other smoking techniques, which allow for the free passage of smoke out of the top of sides of the unit. The smoke has to force its way out of the sides of the lid, causing smoke pressure inside. High temperatures are generated within the Abu and the food cooks in the time it takes for the meths to burn out, which is usually about 20 minutes.

I have no idea just how much heat is generated during the process, but the food smokes and cooks at a far higher temperature than occurs in any other form of hot smoking. Those who deal in mechanical smoking equipment tend to be some-

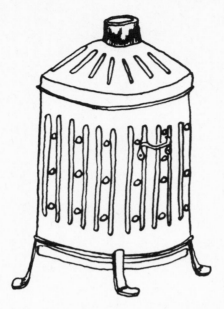

Dustbin incinerator which can be purchased
from hardware stores. A useful ready-made
smoke producing unit

what contemptuous of the Abu, stating that it is impossible
to achieve adequate smoke penetration with it. While I do
have certain reservations about the Abu, I consider that it
produces tolerable smoked trout and sausages and is quick
and foolproof in operation; but there is one job for which the
Abu is unrivalled, which I will go into when discussing smoking
quail.

I have described Abu smoking for, although its possibilities
are limited, you can have a great deal of fun with this device
and it does illustrate the basic principle of all hot smoking
units, having a container for the sawdust, a drip tin to catch
the drips and so keep the sawdust clean, a rack to support
the food, and a source of heat to ignite the sawdust and heat
the chamber sufficiently to cook the product.

Dustbin hot smokers

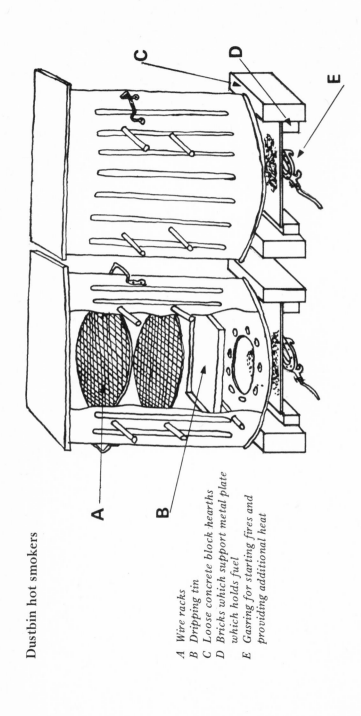

A Wire racks
B Dripping tin
C Loose concrete block hearths
D Bricks which support metal plate
   which holds fuel
E Gasring for starting fires and
   providing additional heat

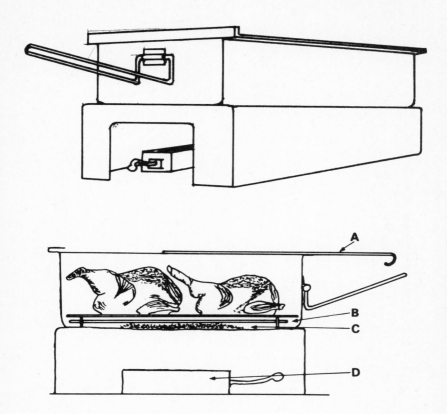

A   Sliding lid
B   Combined drip tin and wire rack
C   Sawdust
D   Meths burner

The Abu pressure smoke box

Ordinary hot smoking kilns

The outside temperature is not a problem for hot smoking kilns as, should the weather happen to be hot, the kiln will simply require less fuel to maintain its correct temperature, which, in my own case, simply means turning the gas down. For trout, mackerel, eels and sometimes quail, pheasants and domestic ducks, I use hot smokers constructed from new, unused galvanized dustbins. The bins are bored at intervals so that 3/8-in. steel rods may be inserted. The first pair of rods support a dripping tin, and higher up three more pairs of rods support moveable wire netting trays. Alternatively, articles can simply be suspended from rods placed across the top of the bins, which are then covered to retain the heat and smoke. Before use, the bins must have smoke passed through them for at least 12 hours, so that tar deposits can settle on the metal, which will prevent the first batch of food from becoming metal-tainted. The bins stand on a hearth constructed of two concrete blocks, standing on their edges. Four bricks inside the blocks support a piece of sheet metal, in my case corrugated iron beaten flat and perforated. It is on this tin sheet that the sawdust is placed. The fire is started by placing the gas ring under the metal plate. The sawdust, which is placed in a neat pile, about half a biscuit-tinful, soon ignites, and then the gas ring is transferred to the top of the plate, directly under the bottom rim of the bin, this bottom having been well perforated with a cold chisel. It is not necessary for the gas ring to be placed dead centre under the bin to ensure an even heat distribution, and in any case the centre of the plate is covered with sawdust, so it is quite in order for the head of the gas ring to rest just under the bin's edge.

Smoke rises upwards through the perforations in the bottom of the bin, and the gas ring heats the interior, but the dripping tin protects the good from the direct heat of the gas flames. A thermometer, protected by a metal case, is introduced into the kiln via a hole bored in the metal near the top of the kiln. When the required temperature is reached, and the food is placed in the kiln, the temperature will drop, then mount again as the food heats through. You must watch the temperature carefully after about an hour, as by this time the sawdust will be smouldering well and will contribute a certain measure of heat, so the gas must be turned down. This is particularly important in the case of fish, which must never cook too rapidly or at too high a temperature. With flesh or fowl this is by no means so important. If racks are used, the food on the top rack will be ready before the stuff on the lower levels. The top rack must be removed and the lower ones brought up a rung. On account of this, I much prefer to suspend the food than place it on frames, since when suspended it all cooks evenly. A dustbin smoker can accommodate four Aylesbury ducks or 1½ dozen trout or 4 dozen quail if racks are used. Trout can be smoked on racks but, being soft and impression-able, take the imprint of the wire mesh which does not detract from their palatability but mars their appearance.

As I do a certain amount of commercial smoking from time to time, I sometimes want to smoke a larger quantity of food than my two dustbin smokers can accommodate. As I was handling a fairly large quantity of ducks, quail and phea-sants at one period, I formulated an idea for a cabinet smoker. I submitted plans to two companies and I was given estimates of £150 and £250 — the price of steel, I was told. Not requiring gold-plated smoking kilns, and as I could have bought a 56-lb capacity mechanical kiln for £350, which would have dealt with both cold and hot smoked products, I decided the estimates were a little steep, so I acquired a dis-used oil cabinet for £2. A blacksmith burned or bored holes where I required them, to allow the exit of smoke, to take supporting rods for racks and dripping tins and to enable me to introduce my ubiquitous gas ring to the interior of the cabinet. The structure was covered, inside and out, with a cellular paint which I burned out by pouring a quantity of methylated spirits into a tray and igniting. Two-thirds of the way up the cabinet was a most convenient shelf, which took four bricks on which I was able to stand a thin steel plate where I could pile my sawdust. A few inches above there was room for dripping tins, then, higher still, shelves constructed of gridweld on which I could place the articles to be hot smoked. The gas ring stayed put beneath the steel plate and its sawdust, and ignited the sawdust and heated the smoking chamber. This is a most efficient piece of equipment and can quickly be heated to quite high temperatures if required. It is particularly economical to use and will function on a very low flame, doubtless assisted by the close proximity of the smouldering sawdust to the product. It will take eight ducks or sixteen pheasants comfortably.

Altogether, I would say my cold and hot smokers have cost about £10 in cash to construct, plus a good deal of labour and a certain amount of ingenuity.

There are doubtless many other things from which a hot smoker could be constructed. Wooden barrels are traditional for the production of Arbroath smokies, and I dare say an old electric oven into which some ingenious person has introduced a stream of woodsmoke could be a useful tool indeed. If it is hot enough and smoky enough, you have got yourself a hot smoker.

The mechanical smoker

While on the subject of smoking equipment, perhaps a further word will not be out of place regarding the mechanical smoker referred to earlier, should any home smoker feel inclined to invest in one of these rather elaborate pieces of equipment.

I imagine that all large commercial fish or bacon smoking concerns in Britain will by now have ceased to use traditioanl equipment and will employ mechanical equipment exclusively. The modern smoker which I am acquainted with is the Torry kiln, which is marketed by Afos Limited, Anlaby, Hull, North Humberside. Some of these commercial kilns are very large, costing several thousands of pounds, but the only model with which the home smoker might need to concern himself is the Torry Mini Kiln. This kiln is based on the same principles as the large commercial smoking units, and has a maximum capacity of 56 lb (approx. 25 kilos).

The main advantage the mechanical kiln has over the traditional models is that precise control of temperature, humidity and smoke density can be obtained. Instead of the smoke rising haphazardly upwards, propelled by natural air currents, it is produced in special hearths situated outside the kiln, is circulated horizontally by means of fans or blowers, and is allowed to pass over the products which are either laid out flat on wire racks stacked one above the other on trolleys, or are suspended on rods. The Mini Kiln has four hearths, and the number of fires in use at any one time depends on the type of cure required. Smoke enters the kiln from the hearths via ducts and is first mixed with air. Temperature is maintained by thermostatically controlled electric heaters, and the humidity of the air can be controlled by altering the amount of air intake. The warm air and smoke are then blown by a fan at an even speed over the products arranged on the trolleys in the smoking tunnel. Baffles ensure that the smoke and air are blown evenly across the tunnel. After passing over the product a proportion of the smoke is led up the chimney, but most of the smoke is recirculated and mixed with fresh smoke and air. Halfway through the smoking process the trolleys are wheeled out and rearranged, as the material nearest to the incoming smoke stream dries out more quickly than the rest.

As the whole smoking process is subjected to rigid control, the Torry Kiln gives a more uniform product than can be obtained by traditional methods. It takes far less time to complete the cure and is not usually so dependent upon prevailing weather conditions.

The Torry Kiln is fitted with instruments to control and measure air speed, humidity and temperature, and a smoke density integrator which controls smoke density, one of the variables of mechanical smoking, according to the product undergoing processing.

The disadvantage of the Torry Kiln, when compared with the traditional kiln, is that it requires more care to maintain it in good working order. Like any other machine, it needs regular cleaning and servicing and tar and dust may be removed at fairly regular intervals.

Other improvised smokers

Various other improvised smokers can be made. A 40 - 50 gallon oil drum is particularly well adapted to this purpose. First of all, one end should be cut from the barrel with either a cold chisel or an oxyacetalene torch. The cut-out section should be reduced in size by further trimmage so that it

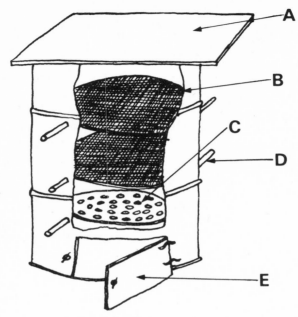

A Loose hardboard cover
B Wire mesh racks
C Perforated baffle
D Rack and baffle support bars ($\frac{3}{8}$ in.
 steel).
E Fire door

Oil drum smoker

finishes up about 3 in. less in diameter. This circular plate should have about 20 holes drilled or punched through it, so that it can later be used as a smoke disperser or baffle. The holes allow some of the heat and smoke through, and the rest of the smoke finds its way around the edge of the smoke spreader.

However, before any further conversion is embarked upon, the oil drum must be burned out, so that no taint of oil remains inside. This is best done by pouring a generous quantity of methylated spirits into a wide flat vessel such as a roasting tin, and placing a large piece of rag in the meths to act as a wick. The oil drum should be placed over the meths,

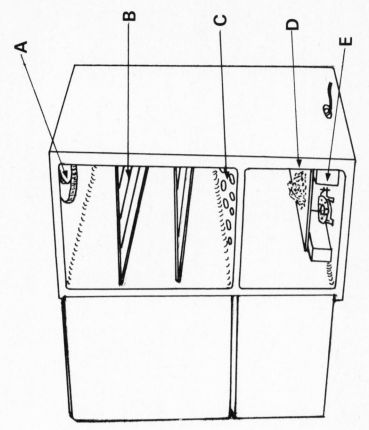

A Roof vent
B Racks
C Smoke spreader
D Metal plate for fuel
E Brick supports

Refirgerator conversion cold smoker

and tilted slightly so there is a 4-in. gap between the ground and the bottom rim of the drum. The meths should be ignited through this gap and allowed to burn out. A similar technique should be employed for the removal of paint from any other metal article which you intend to convert into a smoker, as paint also would taint the product.

To support the smoke spreader, four holes should be drilled in the wall of the drum about 18 in. from the closed end. You can either put long bolts through these holes, securing them by nuts so that about 4 in. of the bolts protrude into the chamber, allowing the smoke spreader to rest upon them, or you can simply position the holes so that two long metal rods can be used as supports instead of the fixed bolts. A series of corresponding holes should be drilled in the wall of the drum so other metal rods can be inserted, their function being to support the smoking racks. Here there are no hard and fast rules. It is up to the individual to decide how many racks there will be and how far apart they will lie, according to the type of food you wish to smoke. I think it is a good idea to make provision for four racks about 5 in. apart. You are then in a position to leave one or more racks out when smoking more bulky objects.

The cutting torch or chisel should then be used to cut a fire hole near the base of the drum. This should measure 12 x 12 in., for easy fuelling and the removal of ash. It should reach right to the base of the drum and leave no edge or lip to hinder cleaning-out operations. It is quite feasible to operate this type of smoker with a permanently open fire hole, but if a hinged door is fitted to the hole this will give you far greater control of draught, heat and smoke.

The racks which will rest on the loose metal rods inside the drum and support the food which is under processing should be circular to give maximum area, and should measure about 1 in. less in diameter than the barrel. The outside rim should be of strong steel and the bottom should be of strong welded mesh about 1 in. square for general purposes, or fine wire screens for smoking of such things as shellfish, nuts or bilberries. A pair of strong handles on either side of the racks will greatly facilitate handling.

To cover the top of the drum use either a sheet of heavy

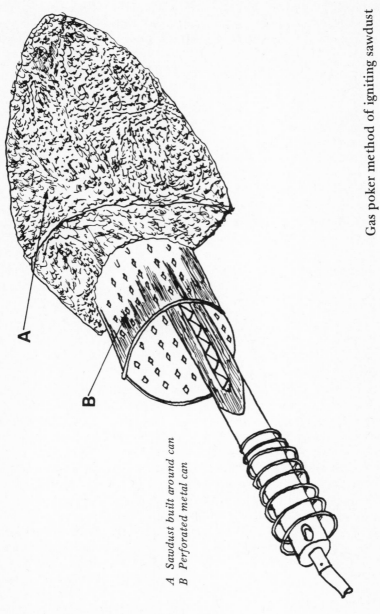

A Sawdust built around can
B Perforated metal can

Gas poker method of igniting sawdust

plywood, a sheet of metal or a piece of asbestos, either flat or corrugated. It is a simple enough matter to insert a stick under this cover in various positions to control smoke and heat escape.

To start the fire, you can stack sawdust around a perforated tin can or a circular kitchen food grater, leaving the nearest end open. If a gas poker is inserted and the sawdust quickly ignites. Alternatively, an ordinary gas ring can be covered with an 8-in. square metal sheet and the sawdust piled around and on top of the plate. When the gas ring is ignited, the covering plate quickly becomes red hot and starts the fire. Once the sawdust is alight, the gas ring can be removed from the sawdust and allowed to burn independently as an additional source of heat should the drum smoker be required for hot smoking.

Refrigerator conversion

An old, disused upright-type refrigerator makes a useful smoker within certain limitations. It is well insulated and so will conserve heat, but, by the nature of its original function, is not designed to stand heat, so it is only suitable as a cold smoker. A hole about 10 in. square or round should be cut in the bottom of the fridge, which should be raised off the ground and supported on a square built of concrete blocks, open at the front to allow the fire to be placed within the square of blocks. Alternatively, the device can be used in conjunction with the remote fire pit and underground smoke tunnel, and as a means of draught control two or three 2-in. holes can be cut in the top of the fridge; better still, it can be fitted with a length of stovepipe, protruding from the top and preferably fitted with a damper.

The shed smoker

A shed conversion makes a very useful cold smoker, one of its major advantages being that it requires hardly any conversion at all and can be used for ordinary storage purposes when not in use as a smoker. Another advantage is that, as a shed is normally built with adequate headroom, there is plenty of space to work in. Racks can easily be suspended from the roof

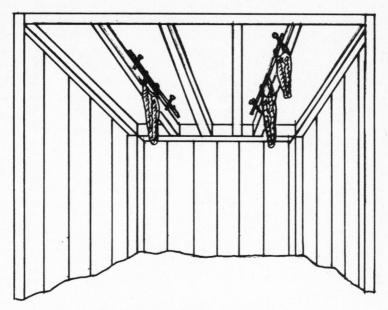

**Fish fillets strung and hung on hazel sticks
supported by 6 in. nails in shed smoker rafters**

or, alternatively, 6-in. nails can be driven into the rafters to
support ½-in. hazel rods. Sides of salmon can be suspended
from the rods by strings threaded under the lug bones (the
hard triangular plates to which the pectoral fins are attached)
and under the shoulder plates, which are situated a few inches
above the lug bones (according to the size of the fish of course)
directly behind the gill covers.

You will need to build a hearth in the middle of the floor
of the shed smoker, which can best be done by using three
sides of a square of loose bricks or concrete blocks as a base,
on which a square sheet of metal should be rested. A three-
sided wall of loose bricks or blocks can be constructed
around the sides of the metal plate to contain the sawdust
or chips. A perforated metal or plywood sheet can be placed
above the fuel to act as a smoke disperser. It is a simple
matter to light the fire by lighting a gas ring underneath the
metal plate of the hearth, which soon becomes red hot and
ignites the fuel.

Various other devices can also be used, including a metal dustbin incinerator. These can actually be purchased ready perforated, for burning garden rubbish. The unperforated kind can simply have a 5-in. hole cut at ground level for draught, with a perforated lid, and are ignited by tilting them on one side, the lighted gas ring being placed under the bottom rim near the draught hole. The only other alteration the shed smoker requires to make it fully operative is a small space (about 2 in. is sufficient) under the door, made by cutting a small amount of wood away, to allow the intake of air. This can easily be covered by nailing a 4-in. board over the gap when the smoker is not being used as such. Most sheds have a space of about 1 in. between the walls and the eaves, which will allow for the escape of smoke, but failing this a few holes can be bored under the eaves.

Another advantage of the shed smoker is that it makes an excellent drying room in which to hang salmon or any other food, after brining and prior to smoking. A disadvantage is that, if smoke should be seen escaping from a wooden shed by a casual observer who is unaware of the operation in hand, the matter might well be misconstrued and the local fire brigade could possibly be called out on a fruitless errand.

8

Cold smoked products

Smoked salmon

There are three varieties of salmon with which we who live in the western hemisphere should concern ourselves. Reputedly king of them all is the Atlantic salmon, the fish which runs up the rivers to spawn in Norway, Finland, Great Britain and Ireland and the rivers on the eastern seaboard of the United States and Canada. This is the fish which is famous the world over as a sporting and culinary proposition and is commonly associated with social prestige and affluence. There is no question that the Atlantic salmon is a very fine fish but perhaps his illustrious connections give him a somewhat unfair advantage over his Pacific cousins.

The main groups of Pacific salmon consist of the sockeye, the pink, the cohoe and the keta, also known as the chum or silverbright. Of these four we can virtually discount the sockeye in Britain as catches of this fish are absorbed by the canning industry. The pink, which can be readily identified by the hump on its back, is seldom seen in this country either except in a tin, so we are left with the cohoe and the keta.

The cohoe is a stocky fish, deep in proportion to its length and lacking the streamlined, torpedo-like form of our own Atlantic salmon. The flesh of the cohoe is a rather deep orangey-pink in colour, deeper hued than the pink flesh of the

Atlantic salmon and somewhat scorned in some quarters on account of its 'inferior' colour. The cohoe is, nevertheless, a very good fish, although very tender to handle when deep frozen and thawed out again. It has a very slightly sweetish taste when smoked which is not at all unpleasant.

The keta salmon is a very similar fish in outward colour and shape to the cohoe, but is somewhat paler fleshed. They are occasionally confused by the commercial packers, as I have sometimes found a cohoe thrown in with a batch of ketas when purchasing salmon for smoking. When this occurs I accept it as a bonus, as the cohoe is higher priced than the keta. The keta has a flesh colour similar to that of the Atlantic salmon, although, all things being equal, it has a lower fat content than the Atlantic and cohoe varieties. Cooked in the traditional manner, it is rather tasteless compared with the other two, but can, with care, make an excellent smoked product. In fact without any attempt at deception on my part, I have frequently had my smoked keta mistaken for Scotch salmon.

If I were to make a choice, I would prefer a *fresh run* Atlantic salmon to any other, but not every Atlantic salmon caught is by any means a fresh run fish. Many rod-caught fish have lain a long time in low water or have battled their way past innumerable obstacles, have lost condition, and are what the smoker terms 'dry fish'. This situation never arises with imported Pacific salmon. All fish are caught by commercial fisheries at the mouths of the rivers, so every Pacific salmon is a fresh run fish and superior in quality to a tired Scottish fish taken late in the summer.

I picked up a very useful tip from an experienced hotelier regarding the treatment of frozen Pacific salmon. As some of the oil is lost during deep freezing, oil must be fed back into the fish to achieve the best results. I do this by painting the fillets with olive oil halfway through the 24-hour air drying period, which falls in between brining and placing in the kiln.

Filleting

A very sharp, thin-bladed knife with a pliable blade is required for this operation. I use one made by J. Marttiini, of Finland,

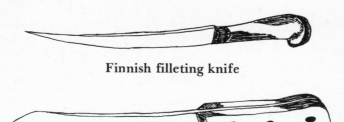

Finnish filleting knife

English fish filleting knife

which is available at most gun and fishing tackle shops.

In the case of whole salmon, the fish must first be gutted, slitting the underside from the vent to the lug bones. The blood channel must then be removed from the back of the gut cavity. The membrane should be broken by the forefinger and the blood channel taken out, preferably under a running tap. There are several large veins present in the belly walls of the fish, and these will turn black during smoking unless punctured and squeezed out. If these veins are ignored, they will not affect the flavour or keeping qualities of the fish but detract somewhat from the appearance.

To fillet the fish, leave the head on as it provides something to get hold of. The neck should be cut through until the spine is reached, as close to the head as possible, leaving the hard shoulder plates intact as these are necessary to assist in the hanging of the fillets or sides. The knife blade should be turned at right angles, so the flat of the blade lies parallel to the length of the spine. You will find it easier if the back of the fish is towards you. A straight cut should be made, slicing through the ribs where they join the spine, cutting the entire length of the fish with the knife blade held all the way at right angles to the length of the body. The large dorsal fin can cause trouble, so the blade must be fractionally raised to pass above this obstacle when it is reached and the same applies to the anal fin lower down. When the first side is freed, the fish should be turned over. This may be harder to remove than the first, as the remaining side has acted as a supporting cushion when removing the first side.

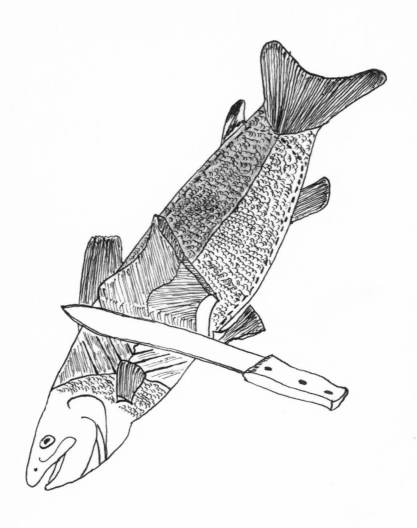

Method of filleting a fish

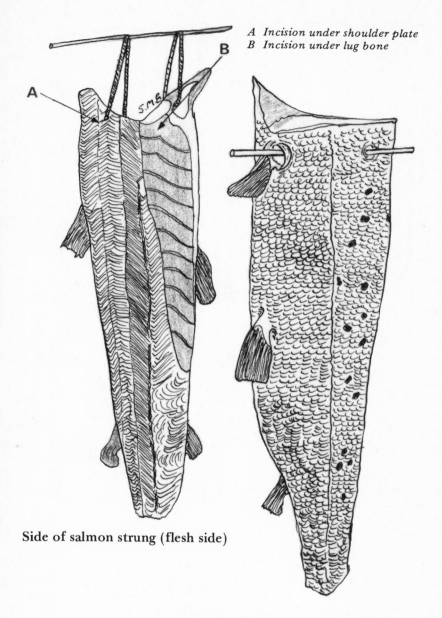

A *Incision under shoulder plate*
B *Incision under lug bone*

Side of salmon strung (flesh side)

Side of salmon strung (skin side)

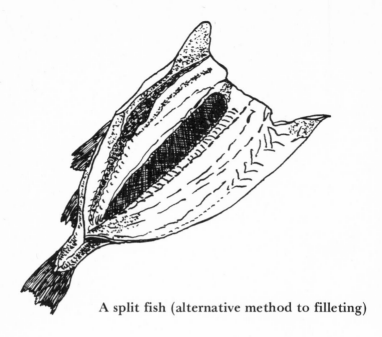

A split fish (alternative method to fileting)

The ribs can either be left intact until the sides are smoked, or can be removed at this stage by taking them out along with a thin layer of flesh. I favour the former course in the case of frozen salmon, as I believe the less the sides are disturbed before smoking the better, to avoid damage.

A slit should be cut behind the shoulder plates and lug bones, through which to thread string to hang the sides by. Some authorities suggest that the skin of the fish should be scored in three places, directly over the thickest parts of the fish to assist salt penetration; but in my own experience this is entirely unnecessary, and undesirable as it disfigures the side.

An alternative method to fileting, which is sometimes preferred in the case of small fish, is splitting. The whole, ungutted fish is split down the back, including the head, and the guts and blood channel are removed, leaving the belly intact. The spine is taken out, save for 3 in. of the tail, which is left to strengthen the fish during subsequent handling, as the fish is smoked suspended by the tail. After pre-salting, a suitable stick is passed through cuts behind the lug bones, to keep the fish opened up. The eyes and gills are also removed.

Pre-salting or brining

If dry salting is favoured, the fish is well washed in cold water, then rubbed with fine salt. The sides are laid on a 1-in.-thick bed of salt in a suitable receptacle. A ½-in. layer of salt is spread on the body of the side, but with only a sprinkling towards the tail. The other side is laid skin down on the first, and another ½-in. layer of salt is spread on top. The time required in the salt obviously varies according to the size of the fish and fat content. Here I find myself at variance with any previous information I have read on the subject. It is suggested that sides from salmon varying between 8 and 24 lb should be salted from 12 to 36 hours. This is far too long; I consider the resulting product to be inedible and would advocate a reduction of these saltings times by half. After salting, the sides should be well washed to remove surface salt and should feel springy and firm to the touch. The fish should then be hung up to drip for 24 hours, preferably at a room temperature of about 65 - 70° F.

During dry salting, the sides will lose 8 - 9% in weight, and wastage through gutting and filleting will probably amount to about 25%.

Brining

This is my favoured method. An 80% brine is prepared (2 lb 10¾ oz of salt to 1 gallon of water) and the sides are totally immersed for periods varying from 1 hour to 3 hours, according to size and fat content, frozen salmon requiring less than fresh fish on account of oil loss. I once prepared a 7-lb September hen fish in poor condition, very red and distended with spawn. I was asked by the clients to salt it lightly, as commercial salt cures always seemed to be too salty for their tastes. I brined this fish for only 50 minutes and this was entirely to their palates.

The brined fish should be hung up, unwashed. In my opinion it is even more preferable to hang the fish up to dry for 24 hours than in the case of dry salted fish, as the sides will only lose 1½ - 3% weight during brining. Brined fish, hung in the manner described, will form a good salt gloss which adds to their appearance.

Smoking

Prior to dry salting or brining, at least one side should be weighed and the weight recorded. The finished product must lose 17 - 18% in weight, so you must do a sum and work out what weight 17 - 18% is of the whole, subtract this from the whole, and the answer is what the smoked side should weigh. So under traditional methods, which depend to a certain extent on atmospheric humidity and ambient temperatures, smoking time required is not therefore a matter of so many hours but until the product has dropped to the correct weight. This is likely to take from 24 to 60 hours and I have even heard of salmon smoking for 4 days. Smoke temperatures should be about 80° F, never higher than 90° F.

Storage

When the salmon has finished smoking, it should not be eaten immediately but should be allowed to mature for at least 24 hours. According to the Norwegians, a salmon should be caught on a Thursday, smoked over the weekend and eaten on the following Wednesday.

Smoked salmon has a fairly good shelf life under conditions of ordinary refrigeration — about a week, with a 10-day maximum. However, it is a commodity which deep freezes particularly well, so there is no need to push it to its limit of keeping time. It can either be cut into pieces, on the skin, or be cut into slices, wrapped in aluminium foil and deep frozen.

Smoked fillets of beef

Some time ago, I had a commercial association with a North Country farmer who, as an expanding sideline, had a smoked food business, supplying many first-class hotels, mainly in the western half of the country. He did not process smoked foods himself but had it custom smoked for him by people like myself. He was particularly keen to put smoked beef on the market — what type or how processed, he did not specify. The idea was left in abeyance for some time, as in any case I was fairly well occupied in smoking ducks, quail and pheasants for him, and it was not until the matter of smoked beef was raised by a first-class butcher of my acquaintance, who had enjoyed my smoked quail, that I pursued the matter further.

As I have already mentioned, the smoking of new products, about which there is no available literature, depends to a great extent on experimentation and intelligent guesswork. It is seldom one gets a new product 100% correct the first time, and beef is an expensive commodity to use as a subject for experiments. I mentioned this point to my butcher friend, who airily waved my caution aside, offering me a box of frozen fillets of beef on which to experiment. For a first attempt, they turned out very well, although at the outset I was not sure whether I should make a cold smoked or a hot smoked product out of them. I did discover that a period in cold smoke was quite sufficient to smoke the fillets right through, and the result was such that I can unhesitatingly recommend that they should be treated as a cold smoked meat and eaten raw, like smoked salmon.

Smoking

The fillets do not require to be of first-class quality. Cow fillets are quite adequate, as are those from cattle which have not been 'done' well in the store period and have finally been finished off on grass, possibly going to market as beef cattle a good deal older than normally would be the case. Such beef is covered with a good layer of fat but the lean is dark and sinewy, without the 'marbling' of fat between the tissues. Although I have not tried them, I imagine that Australian or South African fillets would be quite suitable. Only the thick bottom part of the fillet should be used. The tail end of the fillet tends to go dry during smoking — it is best used for steak Châteaubriand and should be served sliced along the grain, in the Dutch manner, instead of across.

The fillets should be pricked right through with a fork in

Fillet of beef, hung

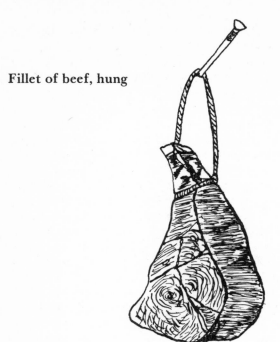

several places on either side, to allow the brine to penetrate. Most of the fat should be removed as this hinders both brine and smoke penetration and, unless the beef has been dead for at least a week, the brine cannot penetrate the flesh and the resulting product will taste comparatively insipid.

The fillets should be covered in 80% brine and allowed to soak for 2½ - 3½ hours, according to thickness and fat content.

After brining, a thin piece of string should be tied tightly around the smaller end of the fillet, about 2 in. from the end, and a loop formed for hanging in the kiln. (See illustration).

The beef should be hung to drip and cure for 24 hours before it is placed in the smoke house. As with all cold smoked products, a beef fillet must lose a certain amount of moisture, and consequently weight, before it can be considered properly smoke cured. The fillets should therefore be weighed before brining, and a calculation made as to what the approximate smoked weight should finally be, working on my principle of a required weight loss of 20 - 25%. During smoking, temperatures must never exceed 80° F or the beef will case harden too rapidly, preventing the escape of moisture. Low smoke temperatures do not appear to make any difference to the final product, but if the beef is smoked at a temperature of 50 - 60° F, it will obviously take longer, as of course it will in times of high relative humidity. Nevertheless I find that 5 - 8 days in the kiln is normally sufficient. It is as well to bear in mind that the fuller the kiln, the longer any product will take, as more moisture has to be evaporated, so it is a good idea never to fill kilns to maximum capacity and to leave a good air space around every article.

The beef will begin to turn black after about 2½ days of smoking, which is as things should be. Beef is a tolerant material and, should the fire go out in the kiln at any time, the product will not suffer until such time as the fire is relit and the flow of smoke begins again. I mention this point as, when a kiln is working for a period of up to a week or beyond, natural human laxity is such that the fire is far more likely to go out than if the kiln should be working for only a couple of days.

Towards the end of the smoking period, the beef should be tested by weighing and, if all seems in order, the final test should be applied. This consists of slicing almost through the fillet at its thickest part, in order to give it the visual test. The freshly cut surfaces should have a dull, matt finish, proving adequate smoke penetration and drying. If the appearance is still bright and shiny, yet the weight loss seems about right, another 48 hours in the smoke will conclude the matter. It is also worth remembering that if either beef or salmon should prove to be particularly stubborn over losing weight during an excessively humid period, they can be taken out of the kiln, allowed to 'sweat' for 12 hours in the case of salmon and 24 hours for beef, then be resmoked until correct weight loss is achieved.

Storage

Smoked fillet of beef has a long shelf life in a refrigerator. It is still good after 3 weeks and could well be considerably longer, particularly in the case of a whole uncut filler, but again I think it is better to wrap in tinfoil and deep freeze as it loses nothing in the process. Smoked fillet forms a hard, savoury rind on its outside which can be eaten or trimmed off according to taste, as in the case of the smoked surface of a side of salmon. In common with other smoked products, beef should be allowed to mature for 24 hours before being eaten, then should be thinly sliced across the grain and eaten as a starter as an alternative to smoked salmon. Lemon juice is a suitable additive, and smoked beef between brown bread and butter is one of my favourite sandwiches.

A smoked fillet, or part of one, can be placed in an oven for 1 hour at a temperature of 240° F, allowed to cool, then be eaten. The result cannot be considered as anything but good but the whole character is completely altered and, for my own palate, I much prefer the cold uncooked smoked beef.

Kippers

The herring, which of course is what the kipper is before it is processed, is seldom the quarry of the sea angler in Britain. The Swedes and the Norwegians traditionally fish for herrings with hand lines from small boats at the mouths of their fjords, often making good catches, particularly when night fishing. Nevertheless, although as a British home smoker you are unlikely to catch your own herrings, if you live close to a port where these fish are landed, you may well decide to smoke your own kippers. If so, you will be able to make certain that you only obtain the freshest of fish.

Smoking

The herrings should first be washed well to remove loose scales, then split from the head, right down the back, and the gut and roe should be removed. After splitting, the fish should be washed again to remove any bits of gut or blood.

Well-conditioned, medium-sized fish should be brined for 15 minutes in 70% brine. Extra large herrings require 20 - 30 minutes and if the fish are lean, eg 'spent herrings' (fish which have spawned), 10 minutes in the brine will be sufficient.

The best way to hang kippers for their pre-drying period and indeed in the smoke house is by employing 'tenter sticks', which are wooden battens fitted with small hooks. However, these are not essential and here a little human ingenuity can be brought in. They should be hung to drip for 1 hour. Longer drying periods are not required, as 'salt gloss' does not play such a large part in the final appearance of the finished product, as gloss in kippers depends to a greater extent on the natural oil within the fish which comes to the surface during smoking.

During smoking, temperatures should be around 80° F, never more than 85° F until possibly the last half hour, when the temperature can be increased to 95° F in order to develop a deeper hue and to bring the oil gloss to the surface of the fish.

Smoking time depends upon the usual factors ie size of fish, quantity in kiln, atmospheric humidity, etc. But as a guideline I can suggest between 6 and 18 hours. As with all cold smoked products, however, weight loss is the surest guide, and from the fresh, split condition the fish should lose 14 - 18% in weight.

Storage

Keeping time is governed by weight loss and varies from 4 to 7 days, bearing in mind that the higher the weight loss, the longer the shelf life.

Smoked cod roes

Cod roes may be processed from either the fresh article or from deep frozen roes. They are extremely delicate to handle, the fine transparent skins rupturing very easily, so their handling is a major part of the technique. They must first be carefully washed in cold water then immersed in 70% brine for about 1 hour.

Smoking

A major problem now is how to suspend the roes for pre-drying and subsequent smoking. If large enough and sufficiently firm, a piece of string can be tied around the bisection of

Cod roe strung for smoking

the roe. If you are in any doubt as to whether the roes will stand this treatment, they can be laid on racks, but a disadvantage of this method is that the roes take the imprint of the racks rather heavily and appearance suffers. Whichever method is used, the roes should pre-dry for half an hour before being placed in the kiln, where they should be smoked at 80 - 85° F for between 12 and 24 hours, according to the usual conditions. The final product is firm, easily sliced and is an attractive dark red in colour. Weight loss should be about 25% of the original weight before brining.

Finnan haddock

Fairly small haddock of about 1 lb in weight are ideal for processing into finnan haddock. The fish must be carefully gutted, as small haddock are very tender and tear easily. The heads are removed and the gut cavity is scraped and cleaned. The fish are then split all the way along the *inside* of the spine, from the neck to the tail fin, care being taken not to cut into the skin of the back. The opened-out fish are then soaked in 80% brine for 7 - 15 minutes, depending on size; a 1-lb fish will require 10 minutes' brining.

After brining they are hung on tenter sticks for about 6 or 7 hours as a good salt gloss is important to the finished product. Haddock are particularly subject to case hardening, so they should be protected from strong drying winds during this period.

Smoking

The finnans should be smoked at 80° F for a period of from 6 to 12 hours, and should be removed before the full colour is reached as this full colour will develop within a few hours of cooling. Required weight loss is 12 - 14%.

There is a slight variation of the process described for the production of 'straws'. Here smaller haddock are used, not in excess of ¾ lb in weight. The preparation is exactly the same as in the case of finnans until brining, which only takes 4 - 5 minutes in the 80% brine. After drying, the fish are smoked from 4 to 8 hours at 80° F, and the final product should have a pale straw colour. Weight loss should be 8 - 12%.

Smoked shrimps

Shrimps can either be cold smoked whole or as peeled meats. For the former method, the shrimps should have the heads removed and are then washed and drained for 30 minutes. They are then brined for 30 - 60 minutes (according to preference) in 40% brine (1 lb 3 oz salt to 1 gallon water), then boiled in the brine or in plain water, again according to taste, for 30 minutes. The shrimps are then allowed to air dry on racks for 2 hours.

Smoking

The shrimps are then placed in the kiln and smoking is carried out for 1 - 1½ hours at a temperature of 80° F. The yield of smoked meats after shelling is approximately 36% of the whole raw shrimp weight.

Alternatively, clean peeled meats may be boiled for 1 - 4 minutes, depending on size, in a 40% brine. They are then allowed to drain on oiled wire mesh trays until the surface of the meat is dry. The trays are placed in the kiln and are smoked for 1 - 1½ hours at 80° F.

Bloaters

Bloaters are produced from whole, ungutted, slightly salted herring, and owe their distinctive flavour to the enzymes or ferments in the gut. The herring are mixed with solid salt for about 12 hours, after which the surface salt is removed by soaking the fish in fresh water for 20 minutes. They are threaded on rods, either through the mouth and gills or through the eyes. As it is not necessary to produce a salt gloss, the fish do not require a dripping and air drying period, and can be placed in the kiln straight away.

Smoking

The total smoking period in the traditional smoke house is about 12 hours (4 hours in the Torry Kiln). The smoking temperature should be maintained at 77° F, and for exactly half the smoking period the bloaters should be dried with an absolute minimum of smoke. For the remainder of the smoking period, very dense smoke should be produced which gives the fish a mild smoky flavour while the product retains a bright silvery appearance.

Storage

The bloaters should only lose about 6% weight, so consequently keeping time is short, about 2 - 3 days.

Red herrings

Besides herring, the raw material may be pilchard and sprat. They are placed in solid salt in a suitable bucket or vat-shaped receptacle for 7 - 8 days, the bulk ratio of salt to fish being about 1:2. Surface salt is removed by soaking in fresh water for 1 hour.

Smoking

The fish are cold smoked for 5 - 6 days at a temperature of 85° F.

Weight loss is 20 - 25% and the fish will keep for several months without refrigeration.

Smoked bacon

Bacon may be cured by either brining or dry salting. The traditional method, either brining or dry salting, appears to vary from one county to another in Britain. For example, dry salting is traditional in the Lincolnshire Fen district, whereas Galloway, in south-west Scotland, favours brining.

The dry cure for meat should be applied at a rate of 1 lb per 10 lb meat. Half the dry cure should be rubbed well into the meat 5 days after killing, no sooner or the meat will not absorb the cure. As pork taints very easily, it is most important that the meat should be kept cool during this waiting period. The other half of the dry cure should be applied after 3 days. The bacon should be allowed to cure at a rate of 2 days per 1 lb of flesh, eg 12 lbs must cure for 24 days, after which time the bacon must be removed from the salt and any of the cure adhering to the surface should be brushed off and the bacon kept quite dry. Bacon cured in this manner would keep at room temperature for considerable periods, suspended from rafters, in the days before refrigeration came into general use.

Sweet pickle brine should be used for a brine cure, and the meat should remain in the pickle for the same length of time, ie 2 days per lb, and should be agitated and turned every 2 days. After brining the bacon should be well washed and hung up to drain in a cool place for 48 hours.

Both dry cured and brine cured bacon is now ready for smoking, if desired. The length of the smoking period varies according to individual taste. Temperatures should be 75 - 80°F and can vary from 24 hours, for a very mild smoke flavour, to 7 days for a stronger smoke cure.

Smoked ham

Ham is thicker than bacon, so penetration by either sweet pickle or dry cure takes longer: 3 days per lb should be allowed. If the brine cure is used, it is a good idea to inject around the bone with the brine pump before the ham is totally immersed in the pickle, after which it should be turned every 2 days and the brine must be stirred. The rule applies about temperature as in all protracted cures, namely that it is far safer to keep it around 35°F. After the curing period, the ham should be washed and hung up to drain at around 38°F for 48 hours.

Like bacon, the time the ham should be smoked varies according to taste. It should be smoked at a temperature of from 70 - 80°F for a period varying from 48 hours to 6 weeks. In the case of the more lengthy period, smoking does not need to be continuous. The fire may be lit intermittently, and during this period slices of ham may be cut off and eaten, the remainder staying inside the smoke house for further smoking. I understand that a similar system was used in old-fashioned chimneys in Germany, which had small doors in them a few feet from the ground for easy access. Smoked sausages and other meat were simply stored in the chimney until required.

Ham prepared in this manner can also be hot smoked at 220 - 250°F, and will require a cooking period of 5 - 7 hours according to size.

Smoked eggs

This is a very little known method, but of all the smoked foods the flavour of smoked eggs is quite unique. New laid eggs should be avoided as they can be extremely difficult to remove from the shell when boiled, so it is better to use eggs which are about a week old.

The eggs should be hard boiled by placing them in cold water and bringing to the boil. When boiling point is reached, the pan should be removed from the heat and allowed to cool for 15 minutes. The water should be drained off, and after the eggs have cooled down the shells should be removed. The eggs are well sprinkled with table salt and white pepper, then placed on wire racks in the cold smoker and smoked at about 80°F for about 12 hours, by which time they should have turned deep amber. They may be sliced and eaten in sand-wiches, served in salads with mayonnaise or used as hors d'oeuvres when dusted with paprika. They are also used in smoked rabbit pie.

Smoked nuts

Most kinds of nuts are suitable for smoking — almonds, either whole or blanched, walnuts, brazils, chestnuts, hazlenuts and pistachio nuts. Nuts should be placed on fine wire gauze screens. Some people say nuts cannot stand heavy smoking and advocate a smoking time of 2 - 3 hours at 75 - 85°F, but this is a matter of taste and I prefer them smoked for 10 - 12 hours.

Smoked cheese

Few people can be unfamiliar with Austrian smoked cheese, a commercially available product in a sausage-like form. During the processing of Austrian smoked cheese, the milk from which it is manufactured is first smoked, then made into cheese, no further smoking process being involved. As cheese making is probably beyond the scope or inclination of the average home smoker, the cheese must be smoked in the piece.

First of all, any rind or protective wax, plastic or muslin coating must be removed. Any kind of mild cheese can be smoked. Danish Blue, Gorgonzola, Stilton and Camembert are not suitable.

To allow for maximum smoke penetration, the cheese should be cut into pieces not more than 1½ in. thick. Smoking is best carried out in the lower temperature ranges — 60°F is ideal. Again opinions vary on how long the cheese requires smoking. In the opinion of some, 2 hours in light smoke is all that is required, but I prefer a period of 5 - 6 hours. After smoking, the cheese should be wrapped in aluminium foil and kept under refrigeration until required, but to obtain the finest flavour from smoked cheese it should be kept at room temperature for about 3 hours before eating.

Smoked bilberries or whinberries

The berries must be firm in texture and not over-ripe, otherwise the keeping qualities of the finished product will be impaired. The berries should be placed on a fine wire mesh rack and cold smoked at 75 - 85°F until they lose moisture and the skins take on a wrinkled appearance, rather like dried raisins. Smoking time will depend on atmospheric humidity and appearance must be accepted as a guide. They should be stored in a refrigerator in a covered but not airtight vessel.

Smoked bilberries are excellent when accompanied by ice cream or clotted Devonshire cream.

Smoked sausages

It would be possible to write a whole book on sausages and still fail to cover the subject in its entirety. So many different types of sausage are made in so many different parts of the world. Recipes vary from county to county, from province to province, and from country to country and from continent to continent.

As this is the case, I do not propose to go too deeply into sausage making, but will describe one type only. For the large manufacture of sausages, special equipment is essential in the form of mincing machines, mixing vats and filling machines. The skins or casings are traditionally of animal composition, requiring careful and specialized handling and storage techniques. It would not be economic for the home smoker to invest in this equipment for what might, for him, be a once-a-year sausage-making excursion. I think the home smoker would be well advised to make do with a minimum of equipment and to enlist professional help, in the form of a friendly butcher, over certain phases of the process.

Certainly you can mince your meat in a domestic mincer, the larger the better, but it would be worth the little extra cost to engage professional help in supplying the casings and filling them from the machine specially designed for the job.

This is the recipe for an excellent smoked sausage.

    6 lb lean beef
    4 lb pork (preferably 50/50 fat and lean)
or   5 lb venison or elk
    5 lb pork (50/50 fat and lean)

1½ oz white pepper
2 oz salt
½ tablespoon powdered garlic
¼ oz whole black peppers
20 fl. oz red wine

The beef or venison is cut into pieces approximately 2½ in. square and placed in a vessel containing sweet pickle brine. Keep refrigerated at 35° F for about 10 days, and agitate and stir well every third day. The meat is them removed, washed, and placed on wire mesh racks to dry, still under refrigeration, for 24 hours.

When the beef has dried thoroughly, the pork is cut into pieces small enough to go into the mincer. Both pork and beef pieces are placed in a large mixing pan. The pepper, salt and garlic powder are added and the ingredients thoroughly mixed.

The meat is now put through the mincer twice, using cutters which will produce a medium to coarse texture. The peppercorns and red wine are now added to the minced meat and the contents of the pan are thoroughly mixed and allowed to stand for 2 days. The butcher should then be asked to stuff the sausages, using casings that will allow for a sausage about 18 in. in length and 2 in. in diameter. The stuffed sausages are left hanging in a refrigerator for 2 days.

The sausages are now ready for smoking. They should be hung in the smokehouse vertically and smoked at a temperature of 85 - 95° F for 14 - 16 hours.

After the smoking process follows the maturing process during which the sausages are kept at 35° F fot 2 weeks. At the end of this period the sausages will have lost about 50% of their original weight. They may now be kept in a cool dry larder or under refrigeration, and are ready to eat without further cooking.

9

Hot smoked products

Smoked trout

There are three varieties of trout which might concern the
smoker. Commonest of all is the rainbow. This fish is the
mainstay of the commercial trout farm, reproducing easily and
growing well under reasonable conditions. It is an ideal fish
for stocking lakes and reservoirs, but will not normally stay
put in rivers. It is an excellent sporting and eating fish with a
delicate flavour and is delicious when hot smoked.

Some trout farms have the American brook trout. This fish
is wider across the back than the rainbow, but shallower in the
body. Its flesh is particularly firm and somewhat rubbery, and
as such is a particularly good subject for the smoker as it does
not easily suffer damage during handling.

The native brown trout is my favourite fish. It has a distinctive, somewhat 'earthy' flavour which I find particularly appeal-
ing, although more conventional palates might well favour
the rainbow. Trout from 8 oz to 1 lb are the best sizes for
smoking.

Smoking

The fish are gutted and the blood channel removed and the
belly cavity well washed under a running tap. Heads are left
on as a means of support during processing. The trout should

Trout pierced through eyes for hanging

be immersed for 1 hour in 80% brine, and after being taken out should be pierced through the eyes with a thin metal rod, as a convenient method of hanging in the kiln. Small pieces of wood, such as broken matchsticks, should be placed between the lug bones of the fish to keep the belly flaps apart, so that the passage of smoke up the belly of the fish is unhindered and the fish is thus able to dry out sufficiently. In the case of a larger fish, it will probably require a second piece of wood lower down the belly.

The trout should be placed in the kiln while wet with brine, and cold smoked at 80° F until the skins are fairly dry. This is likely to take 6 - 8 hours in the traditional kiln. The hot smoking kiln should be pre-heated to 180° F and smoke should be flowing freely when the fish are transferred to it. Temperatures will drop until the fish have heated through, and care must then be taken to maintain the heat at a steady 180° F

Trout pierced through mouth and gill cover

for the final hot smoking period, which takes about 2 hours. If the temperature exceeds 200° F, there is a grave risk that the heads of the trout will come apart, causing the fish to fall to the bottom of the kiln where they will char. Trout are easy fish to smoke, but this can be a problem.

The final product should have a slightly wrinkled skin, golden in the regions of flank and belly. The flesh should be firm and moist with a good smoky flavour. Weight loss during smoking is about 15% but, taking into account gut loss, the total weight loss from the fresh, ungutted trout to the finished product, could be 25 - 30%.

Smoked eel

The size of the eel to be smoked deserves some consideration as small eels are hardly worth bothering with, yielding very little final weight of flesh and tending to dry in the process. An eel with a minimum diameter of 1½ in. is required, larger for preference. If live eels are used, they can be killed by placing them in a container and sprinkling a good quantity of salt over them. This will kill them in about 2 hours and also help to remove a good deal of their natural body slime. As there is, at the present time, such a loud politically motivated outcry against our traditional field sports, it does seem perhaps a little odd that this slow death for eels is officially advocated by the Ministry of Agriculture, and it must be left to the conscience of the individual as to whether this method is permissible. The eels are given a good scrubbing to remove more slime and then are gutted, care being taken to make an incision into the flesh, 1 - 1½ in. *below* the vent, in order that the kidney may be removed to prevent tainting. Heads are left on and the eels are brined in 80% brine. Here there is a great diversity of opinion as to how long the eels should be soaked in the brine. Some authorities advocate as little as 10 minutes, but for a reasonable sized eel I would advise 20 - 30 minutes.

The eels should be pierced with metal rods through the throat from front to back. A few small pieces of wood should be inserted along the length of the body cavity, to keep the flaps apart and assist in drying and smoke penetration.

Smoking

The eels should be smoke dried for a period of about 2 hours at 90°F, then the temperature should be raised to 120°F for half an hour; the final period, when the eels are cooked and finished, should be 1 hour at 170°F. Occasionally, larger eels will require longer at this final temperature and the weight loss guideline is that the fresh, gutted eel should lose 15 - 20% of its original weight. Total weight loss from the whole eel to the final smoked product could be in the region of 40%.

Well smoked eel is a truly gourmet product. It should have

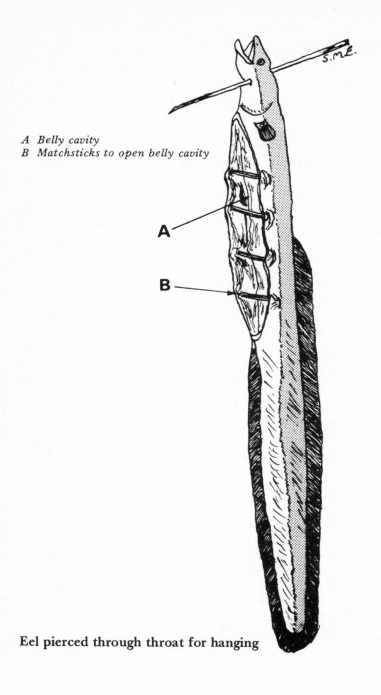

A *Belly cavity*
B *Matchsticks to open belly cavity*

A

B

Eel pierced through throat for hanging

a smoky flavour with only a mild taste of salt. The flesh should be white, firm and buttery, but not rubbery, and is excellent with sour cream as an additive.

Buckling

Traditionally, the buckling is a hot smoked, whole baltic herring. It is highly esteemed in all the Scandinavian countries and Germany but is seldom obtainable in Britain, which is a great pity.

Although tradition states that buckling should be prepared from baltic herring, any good-quality, fresh or frozen herring are quite suitable, no matter which sea they swim in.

Smoking

A brine of 70% or 80% should be used and the fish are brined whole for 2 - 4 hours, with head, guts and milt intact. After brining the fish should be washed in cold water, then pierced through the eyes with rods, in the same manner as trout. They are hung up to dry for 2 - 4 hours, depending on the prevailing humidity.

The temperature in the kiln should be 85° F when the fish are placed inside. After half an hour the temperature should be slowly raised to 160° F and maintained altogether for an hour, giving a kiln drying period of 1½ hours in all. Some fresh sawdust is now sprinkled on to the glowing embers to provide a dense smoke. The buckling ar ethen finished off at a reduced temperature of 140 - 158° F for a period of 1 - 1½ hours, depending on size. Total weight loss should be 20 - 25%.

Smoked mackerel

Considering the large numbers of mackerel which are taken annually around the shores of Britain, not to mention the ease with which they can be caught, it is surprising that smoked mackerel are only just gaining a foothold as a delicacy in this country.

In my opinion, hot smoked mackerel ranks with the very best of hot smoked fish products, and the fact that it is relatively cheap to buy is an added advantage.

Mackerel quickly lose their character once the initial sea freshness has worn off, so it is most important that very fresh fish are used. A mackerel should at all times feel firm and stiff, like a cucumber. Any hint of flaccidity means that the fish is too far gone for human consumption. Ideally, the mackerel should be in the smoker the same day as it is caught, or the following day at the latest, but of course, if they are gutted and frozen this amounts to the same thing.

Smoking

The mackerel should be gutted and the blood channel removed but the heads left on. They should be brined for 1½ - 2¾ hours, depending on size, in a 70% or 80% brine. After brining, mackerel should be washed in cold water, as a salt gloss is not required. They should be pierced through the eyes for hanging and small pieces of wood should be placed in the belly cavity to keep the flaps open, as in the case of eels and trout, to ensure correct drying out and smoke penetration. They should be hung to pre-dry for 2 or 3 hours, then be placed in the kiln for cold smoking, which should take 4 - 6 hours at 80°F, or until their skins are dry. The temperature in the hot smoker should be raised to 180°F and the fish placed inside. Smoke cooking at this temperature varies according to the size of the fish and can take between 2½ and 3½ hours. The appearance of the fish as it cools is an excellent guide. The skin of the belly and flanks should turn a deep golden colour and develop very fine wrinkles, far finer than the wrinkles a smoked trout shows; weight loss should be about 25%. One advantage the smoked mackerel has over some other fish is the ease with which the bones can be removed. After the spine and ribs have been taken out, there is a complete absence of the very fine bones which fish of the herring family seem capable of concealing anywhere.

Arbroath smokies

The Scottish town of Arbroath is famous for two things: the Declaration of Arbroath, when the King of the Scots and his subjects told the King of England exactly what he could do with himself, and Arbroath smokies. These are manufactured from small haddock or whiting which have had their heads removed and their guts pulled out along with the head, the bellies being left intact. They are tied together in pairs by their tails and can thus be suspended over rods for smoking.

Traditionally, smokies were smoked in barrels set over fires and the final product had a dark, tarry appearance which cannot be achieved in modern mechanical kilns.

Smoking

A 70% or 80% brine is used and the fish are soaked from 30 to 45 minutes. They are a lean fish, so salt penetration is more rapid than is the case with fatty fish, like mackerel and buckling.

They should be pre-dried for 2 - 4 hours, then placed in cool smoke (86° F) for half an hour. The temperature is then raised to 160° F and maintained at this heat for a further hour. The fire should then be disturbed and fresh sawdust added to the glowing embers to produce a dense smoke, but the temperature should be dropped to 150° F and maintained for 1½ hours, at the end of which time the smokies are ready. Weight loss should be about 30%.

Hot smoked salmon

This is an alternative method of dealing with salmon which is not widely known in Britain. It should in particular commend itself to anyone fortunate enough to catch a fair number of salmon, and who would therefore be most likely to appreciate another method of presenting them. Fine fish though the salmon undoubtedly is, it is an established fact that a surfeit of it causes one's appetite for it to pall quickly when it is poached in the usual style, and there must surely be a limit to the cold smoked salmon any person would wish to consume. Untraditional as it may be considered, it forms the basis of an excellent salad.

Smoking

The salmon is gutted and the blood channel removed, then beheaded; the lug bones and shoulder plates are removed, as they are not required to hang the fish by. The fish is then cut into segments or steaks, about the size you might expect to find in a large can of tinned salmon. The spinal section is removed from each segment, but the skin is left intact. Each piece of fish is washed in cold water, then allowed to drain for 10 minutes. The pieces are now placed in 95% brine (3 lb 5½ oz salt to 1 gallon water) for 2 hours, then after removal are washed and drained for 15 minutes. The pieces of salmon are now placed on wire mesh trays and allowed to stand for half an hour at room temperature (65 - 70° F) with the skin in contact with the tray. Smoking commences at 80° F and is gradually raised to 170° F over a 3-hour period. This temperature is then maintained and smoking continues for a further period of 2½ hours. The fish is now ready and, as it begins to cool, the skin should be removed.

Smoked pheasants

The idea that it might be a feasible proposition to smoke pheasants was entirely my own. I am not a fisherman myself but I do shoot and consequently have a fair quantity of game through my hands every season.

We are quite fond of pheasants, but after a time we become tired of them. My wife has managed to purloin a recipe from the daughter of one of the hereditary Scottish clan chiefs, which involves doing a roast pheasant up, off the bone, with cream, garlic and button mushrooms and serving the result on a bed of savoury rice. This alters the character of the pheasant completely, to such an extent that it is unidentifiable as pheasant, making a welcome change from pheasant done in the conventional manner. We are not keen on keeping pheasants in deep freeze over the summer. There seems to be something not quite right in eating roast pheasants during the close season, so the idea was formulated that it might be possible to smoke pheasants as an alternative.

There is no question as to the success of smoked pheasants,

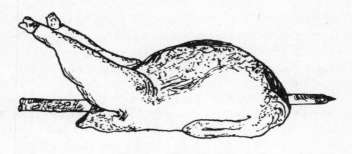

Pheasant or chicken impaled on hazel stick
for smoking

but some care should be exercised over the choice of birds for
smoking. The young, comparatively fatless birds of October
and November are not at all suitable, unless very early hatched
and consequently more mature. I would recommend that the
pheasants shot during the first couple of months of the
season should be utilized in the ordinary manner. Ideally, a
pheasant for smoking should be mature with plenty of fat on
it. Young birds tend to go dry during the process and are not
so full flavoured as the adult birds. An appreciable advantage
of smoking pheasants is that old birds can be utilized, as
smoking tenderizes elderly game, and the final hot smoking
can be slowed down and lengthened until the bird is completely tenderized. A heavy, fat old cock can be ideal — this kind
of bird can be difficult to deal with by other methods: apart
from casseroling him in cider or white wine for several hours,
he is fit for little else.

The pheasants should be hung in the feather for 3 days
before plucking and drawing, and never allowed to become
'high'. They should then be either deep frozen until required,
or processed fresh.

They should be pricked with a fork in the regions of breast
and thighs and covered in brine, weighted down. The brine
can either be 90% (3 lb 1¾ oz per gallon of water) or 80%,
prepared as specified for salmon. If 90% brine is used, the
birds will require soaking for 1¼ hours. They will require 2
hours in the 80% solution.

The birds should be prepared for hanging by fastening a short piece of string to the upper wings, then doing the same with the other end of the string to the oppostie wing, thereby forming a loop. The birds should be hung, wet with brine, to drip and pre-dry for 24 hours. They should either be hung in the kiln by their string loops, or placed on wire racks, in which case one need not bother to string them. I favour the former course as this allows for the free passage of smoke through the interior of the bird, which should have an opening at the neck end. The pheasants should be cold smoked for a period of from 24 to 48 hours, according to the size and condition of the birds. The larger and fatter the birds, the longer I suggest they are given the cold smoke. It does not matter if smoke temperatures in the kiln are low, say 50°F, but they should not exceed 80°F. Any birds which appear rather lean will benefit from the application of a painting of olive or vegetable oil over their skins. After cold smoking the birds should either be hung in the hot smoker by their string loops or placed on their backs on wire racks.

As pheasants tend to be rather dry fleshed birds, I believe it is wise to avoid excessively high temperatures during hot smoking. I regard as ideal 180 - 190°F for a period of 3 - 4 hours, depending on age.

After smoking, the pheasants should be cooled on wire trays and allowed to mature for at least 24 hours before any attempt is made to eat them.

Smoked pheasants are ideal as a meat base for summer salads and make a first-class filling for sandwiches. In fact I can think of nothing better when grouse shooting than sandwiches containing smoked pheasant from the previous season. They have a very delicate flavour and highly flavoured additives should be avoided. Horseradish will effectively mask their flavour and should not be used. Only a little lemon juice should be added, or even nothing at all.

Storage

They have a shelf life under ordinary refrigerated conditions of 10 - 14 days and lose nothing in quality if deep frozen for many weeks, provided they are wrapped in tin foil.

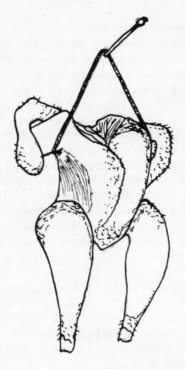

Turkey, chicken or pheasant strung by wings

Smoked quail

There are three varieties of quail in Britain. There is the European quail which occasionally spends the summer and early autumn here, sometimes breeding successfully before migrating back to the continent before winter sets in. For many years, even before the Protection of Birds Act came into being, the quail has been a completely protected bird in Britain, which is no bad thing considering the persecution they suffer at the hands of our French and Italian neighbours.

Next we have the American bobwhite quail. This is an excellent sporting and eating bird, and is virtually the mainstay of all inland game shooting activities in the USA. They do well in the wild state under favourable climatic and ecological conditions and are fairly easy to rear, so wild stocks can always be augmented should the level of a local population decline for any reason. The bobwhite is a sedentary species and has occasionally bred in the wild in Britain after being released, although our climate is hardly suitable for it to gain a firm enough foothold to become recognized as a resident breeding species.

Lastly we have the Japanese or coturnix quail. To the best of my knowledge, this is not a Japanese wild bird but a commercially manufactured article, created by the Japanese from a foundation of the quail which abounded in millions in the Middle East and many other hot countries in biblical days. The Japanese quail was the original battery hen and was kept in a tiny individual cage with scarcely room to turn round. Under these conditions, a quail would sometimes lay over 365 eggs in the course of a year. The Japanese quail matures at 6 weeks, when it will commence to lay eggs, which will be fertile when the bird is 7 or 8 weeks old.

This quail is the most prolific of the entire, rather extensive quail family, which of course commends it to the commercial producer. As it matures so quickly, it shows an excellent food conversion ratio, probably greater than in any other form of livestock kept by man for food.

It is the Japanese quail which is served stuffed and roast, on a bed of pâté, in the best restaurants of Europe, so as it is the most readily available quail, this is the one we must concern ourselves with. Smoked quail will not be found in many restaurants, and I came across it quite by chance in a hotel in Lancashire. This was in my early days of smoking when I was playing about with Abu smoke boxes. By trial and error (especially the latter) I produced a more than tolerable product in the Abu, but as I was asked to smoke a fairly large quantity of quail for a commercial establishment, I realized that I would need to devise a method of smoking the birds which would deal with them in quantity. Here the situation differed from my own private ventures. The quail I originally dealt with were prime, 6-week-old roasting birds, but my business colleague wanted me to smoke his old ex-laying birds, the bulk of whom were large and fat, some weighing 8 - 10 oz dressed, while some were fatless and sinewy, yet all required converting into prime smoked quail.

The method I evolved is as follows. I would prick the quail on either side of the breast to allow the brine to penetrate the flesh more easily. I would soak the birds for an hour, making certain each body cavity was completely filled with brine, so that it could penetrate from within also. After brining, I would wash them well and allow to drain on racks for 3 hours. The next stage was an overnight stay in the cold smoker with smoke temperatures at 60 - 80° F, after which I would stack them in the dustbin-type smoker on wire netting racks on three different levels. The sawdust by this time would be well ignited, and the gas ring placed directly under the bin. The temperature would be raised to 180 - 200° F and the birds would cook for 3 - 4 hours. Invariably, the top rack would turn a deep reddish brown before the lower levels were cooked, so these would be removed and the lower racks moved up a rung, until they, too, were finished in their turn. This worked very well for a time although I found there was no way to prevent the lower part of the legs going hard and dry.

I was never completely satisfied with this method, or for that matter the rather too elderly merchandise I was handling, which differed from old pheasants in that the latter have sufficient fat and flesh on their bones to prevent their going dry.

However, this contract eventually finished and from there on I was only concerned with my own enterprises, supplying a few birds to hotels and a good many to shooting men who visit our area. I went back to the 4-oz-plus young roasting birds, and decided on a foolproof technique of processing.

I now brine the birds for an hour but do not prick, as brine can penetrate tender young birds without this assistance. I wash and drain for 3 hours, then give them their 12 hours in smoke at 60 - 80° F. They are then finished in the Abu. As they have been well smoke dried already, the Abu burner only requires a single fill of meths to complete the job, taking approximately 20 minutes, provided only two quail are placed in the Abu at any one time. The quail done in this way are superb. They are well smoked and thoroughly cooked, but the final process keeps them very moist and succulent. The smoked quail certainly deserves to be a great deal better known than it is at present, and is one of the best starters one could ever find.

Smoked grouse

I do not feel there is ever any justification for smoking young grouse. Even in the really good grouse years, young grouse are never all that plentiful, compared to the hundreds of thousands of young reared pheasants which are killed and eaten annually. To me, a young grouse remains so much of a delicacy in its own right that there is no need to look any further for additional means of presentation than the traditional ways of cooking, as advocated by Mrs Beeton and her successors.

Old grouse are, however, a different matter. Unsuitable for roasting by ordinary methods, they can only be casseroled or made into game pie. I do not decry the grouse served in these particular ways but as there is surely a limit to one's appetite for pies and casseroles, smoking offers a feasible alternative as an outlet for over-yeared birds, in fact, in my opinion, it is the best use to put them to of all.

Smoking

As I have advocated all along, game for smoking should never be allowed to hang until it goes 'high'. The grouse is certainly no exception to the rule and should be prepared within 2 or three days of killing. The birds should be well washed inside after drawing and should be pricked with a fork, twice on either side of the breast, right down to the bone. They should be soaked in 80% brine for 1 hour. Grouse, being lean, fatless birds compared with pheasants and quail, absorb the salt readily so do not require too long in the brine. After brining they should be washed inside and out and be allowed to pre-dry on racks for 6 hours; to prevent the grouse drying up during the smoking process, the birds should be liberally rubbed all over with olive or vegetable oil before being placed in the cold smoker. I recommend a period of 36 hours at a smoke temperature never exceeding 75°F, in fact 60°F is better. They can be hung as described in the section on smoked pheasant, with a loop of string attached to their wings, or placed on their backs on wire trays. After cold smoking, they will require oiling again and the hot smoker should be allowed to reach a temperature of 180°F. The birds will require smoke cooking for a period of 3 - 3½ hours at this temperature. Higher temperatures are not recommended, as it must at all times be the object of the operator to avoid excessive drying of a naturally dry bird. The finished product is quite an object to behold. Dark mahogany in colour and displaying an attractive oil gloss, it resembles nothing so much as smoked venison. The smoked birds should be left for a day before eating, when it will be possible to slice them wafer thin if desired as they are firm and close grained in texture and resemble smoked venison in flavour as well as appearance. Only the breasts should be used, as the legs waste away to nothing.

Smoked domestic duck

One of the greatest culinary mysteries of all times, to me, is the fact that smoked Aylesbury duckling is virtually unknown in Britain. Why this is so I cannot imagine. Turkeys, ducks, geese and chickens have been eaten in this country for a very long time, and whereas smoked chicken and turkey cannot be described as common fare, the majority of the more sophisticated type of diner have at least heard of them. With regard to ducks and geese, the smoked versions appear to be almost unknown. I have only once ever seen smoked geese, apart from those I have done myself. This was in the early 1950s at the home of a Ukranian ex-Cossack who was married to a Lithuanian. A few people have heard of smoked duck and vaguely murmur something about 'Ferndown' in Sussex. I have been told on good authority that only at this place in Sussex are smoked ducks produced commercially.

Few commodities lend themselves to smoking as well as the domestic duck, provided one is careful at one stage of the process. They are tolerant in the extreme, are very hard to dry up on account of their large amount of natural fat, and are very, very good to eat. I have smoked ducks commercially for a middleman, who appeared to be able to sell them very well, but I have never managed to build up any sort of a clientèle in this direction.

I have always been very fortunate regarding my raw material, as there lives in the county of Cheshire a very clever livestock breeder. Some years ago he obtained a nucleus of Japanese quail from a breeder in the north, and within a few generations he had improved the stock by selective breeding and improved feeding techniques so that his present-day stock are far superior in shape and flesh to bone ratio than the birds of his original supplier. He has done the same with the ducks. He only keeps a pure Aylesbury, without any addition of Pekin blood, which can increase the size but also the fat content of the duck. Unlike some breeders, he has retained the keel, or breastbone, in his ducks, whereas some producers have, through either negligence or design, allowed the keel to become almost bred out of their birds. The advantage of the mallard-shaped, keeled ducks is that the depth of this bone allows the bird to develop more muscle, or red meat, on the breasts, so increasing the meat to bone ratio of the bird.

I was asked by my original purchaser to smoke the largest ducks for him that I could obtain, so for quite a period I operated with 5-lb-plus ducks. There were quite satisfactory but fat content tended to be high on ducks of this size, and one day my supplier asked me to experiment with some of his 4-lb-plus ducks, to see how they worked out, as he thought he had an outlet for smoked duck. I decided that a duck of 4 lb 5 oz, including giblets, was ideal. There is an initial giblet loss of about 8 oz, leaving a carcase weight of 3 lb 13 oz and a smoking and cooking loss of 11 - 13 oz finally provides a 3 lb smoked duck.

Smoking

The ducks are well and deeply pricked in the areas of breast, thighs and lower legs, and are immersed in 80% brine. Two and a half hours appears to be about right for the 4-lb-plus birds, while birds 1 lb heavier will require 3 - 3½ hours. Their high fat content appears to inhibit salt penetration to a certain degree, but they seem to absorb the salt through the body cavity. After brining, they are strung across the wings and are hung up to pre-dry for 24 hours. Now the tricky stage of the process is reached. Unlike many things, ducks cannot be cold smoked for long periods, yet theoretically, being fat birds and smoke-resistant, they need an appreciable period in smoke. Leave them in too long and they will turn rancid and dangerous to eat. With smoke temperatures of 75 - 80° F they should be given exactly 36 hours in the smoke. If ambient temperatures are low and smoke temperatures do not exceed 60° F, they can be safely smoked for 42 hours. Hot smoking can finally be conducted at temperatures ranging between 180° F and 240° F, the birds requiring 2 - 5 hours depending on size and temperature. This is the point at which the birds show their tolerance of varying techniques. They should be either suspended on sticks in the dustbin-type smoker (four to a bin) or placed flat on their backs on the shelves of a cabinet-type kiln.

The former method is preferable as the duck can drain as it cooks, whereas when the bird lies on its back, liquid fat forms within the body cavity and is liable to deluge the operator when he finally removes it from the kiln, unless great care is taken. Ducks which are suspended by the wings will need their wings pressed back into place while still hot from the smoker, or appearance will suffer. Ducks which have been finished on their backs should ideally be hung up to drain. In any event, ducks are messy creatures to handle on account of their fat content, and should be dried off with paper towelling. Great care must be taken during hot smoking to ensure that every drop of fat from the birds falls into a drip tin and cannot possibly come into contact with a naked flame. Molten duck fat is highly combustible, igniting with a vivid flash which can in turn ignite the ducks themselves, causing them to burn like roman candles. As I have remarked before, smoking is to a certain extent a process of trial and error, and as far as ducks catching fire goes, I have made my errors.

One of the notable features of all smoked foods, which I have not previously mentioned, is that of aroma. Just as a good wine or a fine brandy has its distinctive bouquet, so should every smoked product have its aroma. The smoked duck has its aroma *par excellence*, and coupled with its beautiful deep red-gold colour, it makes one of the most attractive as well as one of the most delicious, of the entire smoked range.

Smoked woodcock

Woodcock are something of a delicacy at any time. They are not normally obtainable in any significant numbers and, roasted on toast in the traditional manner, are appreciated by sportsmen gourmets.

However, I can thoroughly recommend smoked woodcock, and one or two can easily be smoked alongside other species, such as pheasants or quail. When in good condition the woodcock is a fat, moist bird and will retain a good proportion of moisture during smoking.

Smoking

The woodcock should be gutted, as any other bird (the innards are normally left in during other culinary processes). They should be soaked in 80% brine for 1 hour, then allowed to dry on a rack for 3 hours. They are cold smoked at 70 - 80° F for 12 - 18 hours, then hot smoked for 2 hours at 200° F. Alternatively, being small, tender birds, they can be finished off in an Abu smoke box after cold smoking; the time required for a burner of meths to burn out is sufficient to complete the process.

Smoked turkey

Smoked turkey is rather better known, even to the conventional British, than many of the products I have described. Being large birds, with thick layers of muscle, they do not absorb smoke too readily, but on the other hand are not inclined to go dry during smoking. I have never attempted a very large bird, and I would say turkeys from 6 to 10 lb dressed weight are ideal. A bird of this size should be deeply pricked with a fork in all fleshy areas to assist brine penetration, then should be soaked in 80% brine for 4 - 5 hours, depending on size. The bird should be weighted down to ensure that it is covered in brine at all times, and a convenient method is to place a fairly large stone within the body cavity of the bird. After brining, the turkey should be strung across the wings for hanging and should be allowed to drain for 24 hours. Before being placed in the kiln for cold smoking, make sure that the bird is well opened at the neck end, so that the smoke can pass freely through the interior of the bird.

Smoking

In order to impart a good smoky flavour to the bird, it is advisable to give it quite an appreciable period in cold smoke, say 4 - 7 days at a smoke temperature of 60 - 80°F. After cold smoking, it should be hot smoked for a period for 4 - 6 hours, depending on the size and age of the bird, at a temperature of 200 - 220°F. I mention age specifically, as turkey hens which have laid for a season can be a very good buy. They are much cheaper than the young roasting birds and are quite suitable for smoking provided one gives them an extra couple of hours or so in the hot smoker.

Smoked chicken

Much of what I have written about turkeys applies to smoked chicken. Although I have never tried one, I dare say an old boiling fowl could be considerably enhanced by smoking, bearing in mind that it will require a longer hot smoking period than a young roasting chicken. A 4-lb (dressed weight) chicken should be pricked in the same manner as a turkey and should be soaked in 80% brine for 2½ - 3 hours.

Smoking

Chickens should be allowed to drain for 24 hours before cold smoking, and should be left in the kiln from 48 hours to 4 days at 60 - 80°F. A point to be considered in relation to both turkeys and chickens is that, unlike ducks, they will not go rancid during an extended cold smoking period, so this can be somewhat elastic. They will require about 2 hours' hot smoking at 220 - 240°F to complete the process.

Smoked venison (red and roe)

Red and roe venison can, for all practical purposes, be dealt with together. The treatment is identical, the only differences being in brining and cooking times on account of the differences in size and weight. Only the haunches and saddles are suitable for smoking as the more frontal areas have not sufficient depth of flesh; in fact the saddle of a roe has only just enough depth of flesh to render smoking a viable proposition.

Venison should have hung a minimum of 1 week before brining, but on no account should it be allowed to go 'high'. A haunch of roe will require brining for 3 hours in 80% brine, a saddle of roe 2 hours, whereas a haunch of red deer will require 6 hours in the brine and a saddle from the same animal will need 3½ hours in the pickle. I am assuming that the red deer venison will come from ordinary hill beasts, and it is surely a matter of commonsense that a haunch from one of those monsters from Thetford Chase would require considerably longer in the brine.

Whether red or roe, haunch or saddle, venison requires pricking well all over to assist brine penetration. After brining, venison should be allowed to drip for 24 hours. A haunch should be hung by the hock and a saddle should have an incision made in the thin, membraneous flesh between the two ribs which should be included in the saddle when cutting up the beast, and a string loop introduced.

Smoking

Venison is a product which requires to be well smoked to obtain the best results. Roe venison should be cold smoked for about 7 days at a temperature of 60 - 75°F. After 3 days it will begin to turn black, which is as things should be. Red venison should smoke from 7 to 10 days, at similar temperatures. After cold smoking, the femoral artery on the inside of the haunch should be sought and carefully squeezed towards the cut end of the haunch. A small quantity of greenish, rather unpleasant fluid will be squeezed out and should be wiped away with a tissue.

The surface of the venison will now be dry and rather hard, and should be rubbed all over with olive or vegetable oil before being placed in the hot smoker. It can be placed flat, like a joint of meat, on a rack, and roe venison should be hot smoked for 2 hours at 220°F. Red venison will require smoking for 3 hours at this temperature. It is much drier in character than roe and great care must be taken not to over-cook or quality and character will suffer. On no account must smoked venison be eaten until it has aged at least 24 hours. A hard, thin rind will form which I discard after slicing. The venison above the joint should be carved against the grain towards the bone, the meat below the knee joint being carved downwards along the grain.

Smoked venison is so good that it is a matter of some concern, if not annoyance, to me, that at the moment it is only enjoyed by Scandinavians, Germans and Dutchmen in Europe and possibly Red Indians across the Atlantic. Deer stalking in Scotland is of course traditional, but the sport of woodland stalking is now gaining momentum in very many parts of the country, with roe, Sika and feral fallow as the main quarry. These woodland deer are now becoming regarded as a national asset instead of vermin and are a potentially valuable addition to the nation's larder, but as yet venison is not fully appreciated in this country.

Venison (sweet pickle cured, hot smoked)

This method is well adapted to dealing with haunches or saddles of venison from a particularly old red deer, whose flesh will probably be very tough and dry.

If desired, the sweet pickle brine can be injected from the brine pump into the thickest parts of the flesh, right down to the bone. The meat is then placed in a crock under refrigeration and allowed to remain in the sweet pickle for a period of 5 - 7 days for a saddle and 10 - 14 for a haunch, depending on size. The meat should be turned over every couple of days and the brine should be given a good stir at the same time. After brining, the venison should be washed and allowed to dry under refrigeration for a period of 24 hours for a saddle and 48 hours for a haunch. Opinions vary on how long the meat should be cold smoked, but it is my own policy never to hurry a smoking process. I recommend that the venison should remain in the cold smoke for 10 - 14 days, by which

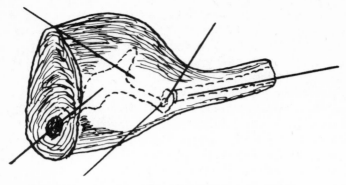

Ham or venison haunch showing injection sites

time it will have acquired that attractive surface blackening.

In the case of the haunch, the inside of the thigh should be squeezed towards the pelvic bone and the small quantity of greenish fluid from the femoral artery should be wiped away. This substance is probably perfectly harmless but, personally I would rather get rid of it.

Smoking

The venison should be placed in the hot smoking kiln after its surface has been well oiled, and should be smoked at a temperature between 200°F and 225°F for 2 hours for a saddle and 3 hours for a haunch.

I must again stress that you should never attempt to cure and smoke venison which has been dead for less than a week, otherwise it cannot absorb the pickle fully and the flavour will be impaired.

Smoked capercaillie

The traditional Scottish recipe for this, the largest of the British and Scandinavian game birds, states that as soon as possible after the bird has been killed, the crop should be removed, the feet cut off and the bird then buried for a fortnight, by which time one should have forgotten where the bird has been buried. This implies that the caper is pretty ghastly fare, but this is an exaggeration, and similar defama-tory statements are often made about the black grouse and its female counterpart, the grey hen, which I and many others consider excellent eating.

Certainly the crop of the caper should be removed as soon as possible after the bird has been shot. It is most likely to contain conifer sprigs which can impart a rather resinous flavour to the flesh if not removed. Certainly nothing appears to be gained from the removal of the feet.

In common with all game birds which are to be smoke cured, the caper should not be allowed to 'hang' for any length of time: 3 - 4 days is quite sufficient! After plucking and drawing, the caper, being a heavily fleshed bird, should be well pricked in the breast and thighs to let the pickle enter easily.

A hen bird should be placed in sweet pickle under refrigera-tion for 4 - 5 days. Cocks are considerably larger and will require 6 - 10 days in the brine, according to size and age.

After brining, the bird should be well washed and allowed to dry off in a refrigerator for 36 - 48 hours, after which it should be cold smoked at 70 - 85°F for a period of 4 - 6 days. Hot smoking should be carried out at 225°F for about 2½ hours if the bird is young, but an old bird is best finished off at 200°F for a period of about 4 hours, or even longer if the thigh is still tough when tested with a fork. This process should completely mask any peculiar natural flavour which the individual might find not to his taste if the bird is simply cooked in the conventional manner.

Smoked octopus

Octopus is sometimes served as one of the courses of a gourmet meal, or occasionally as a starter to a less opulent meal. Cooked by ordinary methods it tends to be rather tough and tasteless, but it is a seafood which can be enormously improved by smoking. Unlike other seafoods, octopus is tough and rubbery and in some restaurants tends to remain so after cooking, but the following process will completely tenderize it.

The body should be cut open and the ailmentary tract

removed. The octopus should be boiled until a pointed instrument can easily pierce the flesh of the tentacle. The octopus should be allowed to cool and, if a large specimen, the dark skin should be removed as this will be too tough to eat. If the octopus is a small one, say 4 - 5 lb, this dark skin is quite edible. The tentacles should be sliced crosswise into slices about ½ in. thick. The body should be cut into pieces of comparable size.

The pieces are put in special octopus brine for 1 hour. After removal from the brine, allow them to drain until dry. They are then placed on oiled wire grids inside the smoker and are smoked at a temperature of 130° F until they become golden brown.

The octopus is now ready for the table but an interesting variation of the process, for those who prefer a fuller flavour, is to oil the octopus. The smoked sections of octopus are placed in a large glass jar with a screw lid, such as a sweet or pickle jar, and a quantity of olive oil is added. The jar should be rotated end over end until the pieces are all coated in oil. After a short time, the oil will be absorbed, so more oil should be added and the jar rotated again. This process should be repeated until the octopus is saturated in oil and will absorb no more.

The oiled octopus is now ready to eat and will keep under refrigeration for several days. Alternatively, it may be bottled in sealed jars.

Smoked oysters

Fresh, live oysters only must be used. The shells should be well washed to remove any traces of mud or sand and the oysters should then be steamed in a cooker for between 20 and 30 minutes. The meat is then taken out of the now opened shells and soaked in a 50% brine (1 lb 8½ oz salt per gallon of water) for 5 minutes. It is a good idea to cut the largest oysters lengthwise before brining to assist salt penetration. The oysters should then be placed on wire racks to drain for 15 minutes before placing in the kiln, which should be pre-heated to 170° F.

Smoking

The oysters will only require smoking for a total period of 30 minutes and should be turned over halfway through the smoking process to give a uniform cure.

Smoked razor clams

Razor clams should first be steamed for 10 minutes to open them. The meats should be shaken out and the clams should be cleaned by removing the stomachs and splitting open the necks. They should then be washed and cut into sections. The clams should be soaked in 60% brine (1 lb 14 oz salt to 1 gallon of water) for 5 minutes, then rinsed in cold water and drained on racks for 15 minutes.

Smoking

After draining, the meats should be placed on wire racks, oiled with vegetable or olive oil and smoked in very light smoke for 30 minutes at 105° F. Dense smoke should then be produced and the clams should be smoked for a further 2 hours in this smoke. For the last 30 minutes of the process, smoking should be carried out at a temperature of 170° F. Weight loss should be 25 - 30%.

Smoked partridge, chukor and ogridge

The grey partridge is a familiar bird in Britain and Europe. Latterly its fortunes have declined in Britain, but its status is now improving owing to the increased awareness of shooting enthusiasts that the species needs help in the form of rearing programmes.

The red-legged or French partridge has always remained in a cliff hanging position, thriving well in some areas yet seemingly incapable of gaining a foothold in some parts, even though helped by man.

The chukor is a handsome bird, resembling a large French partridge in appearance. It is an Asiatic and Balkan species, not as yet appearing in the wild state in Britain, but it is bred on one or two game farms purely as a table bird and is also crossed with the French partridge to produce the ogridge, a made-up name for a man-made bird, which is now being released as a sporting bird.

All these birds are particularly suitable for smoking and, in common with all game birds to be smoked, they should not be hung until they become 'high' or 'gamey'. The chukor is naturally frozen by the producers, within 24 hours of killing, so can obviously be guaranteed fresh enough for smoking when it is purchased.

My own attitude to young grey partridges is similar to my ideas on young grouse, namely that they are really too much of a rarity in most households to justify any other treatment than conventional cooking methods. However there is a strong case for smoking the over-yeared birds which one would normally casserole or put in a game pie. My sentiments differ somewhat on the French partridge. The young birds are not so fine-fleshed or delicately flavoured as their grey or 'English' cousins, and can be mass produced on game farms fairly easily, so I can see nothing against smoking them.

A word on distinguishing old from young partridges is appropriate. The first flight feather on a young grey partridge is V-shaped at the tip. This feather on an old partridge is U-shaped. A young French has a very thin, cream coloured tip to the first flight feather, about ¼ in. in length. The old bird has no such tip.

Grey or French partridges and ogridges should be placed in 80% brine for 1¼ hours. The chukor, being a larger bird, requires soaking for 1½ hours. After rinsing in cold water, the birds should be allowed to dry for about 8 hours. Cold smoking at 70 - 85° F should be carried out for 12 - 18 hours, depending on species, the chukor of course requiring the longer period. The birds will now need oiling with vegetable or olive oil before being transferred to the hot smoke oven.

For old birds, the smoke oven should be pre-heated to 200° F and smoking maintained at this temperature for 2½ - 3 hours. Young birds should be hot smoked at 210 - 225° F for a period of 1½ - 2 hours, giving chukor 15 minutes longer.

10

Smoke roasting

The traditional smoked foods of Britain and Europe are not normally eaten straight from the smoker. In all cases it is usual to allow the food to 'amture' for at least 24 hours after smoking, so that the best possible flavour can be enjoyed. Hot smoked foods are almost invariably eaten cold, as are some cold smoked delicacies such as salmon, cod roes and fillets of beef. Others, like kippers, cold smoked mackerel or finnan haddocks, not to mention ordinary smoked bacon, are cooked before eating, but even these products are not used straight from the smoker.

Almost unknown, then, in Britain and Europe, but common enough in America, are the smoke roasting processes, in which meat or fowl is seasoned and slow roast in a smoky atmosphere at temperatures normally between 200°F and 225°F but never over 250°F. Higher temperatures are likely to case harden the meat, leaving the interior underdone, so the process must never be hurried by using higher temperatures than those recommended. when smoke roasting, the oven should always be pre-heated to the required temperature so that the meat begins to cook right away. The smaller the pieces of meat, the quicker they will cook but they will also tend to dry unless care is taken: after seasoning (see below), they should be well coated in olive or vegetable oil, or have pieces of fat bacon laid over them. Any type of hot smoking oven is suitable for smoke roasting, but an interesting piece of equipment which is very convenient and easy to use is the wheelbarrow smoker.

A steel wheelbarrow should have a 4-in. layer of sand or small stones put in the bottom. An oven grid is supported by bricks or concrete blocks, to stand about 1 ft above the bed of sand; better still is a specially constructed barbecue grid standing on its own legs. A charcoal fire is lit under the grid, and, when glowing well, sawdust is placed at one end of the coals to provide smoke, but not in such quantity that the charcoal is covered and therefore unable to give off sufficient heat to cook the meat. The fish or meat, well oiled, should be laid on the grid, and a sheet of aluminium foil formed into a cone-shaped cover which is then fitted around the grid to cover the food. A few holes should be made near the point of the cone to allow steam and smoke to escape.

According to wind and weather conditions, it may be necessary to build a shield of tin or bricks around the grid to conserve the heat and to prevent the smoke being blown away by a strong wind. Halfway through the cooking process, the cone should be temporarily removed and the meat or fish turned to ensure even cooking.

Basic seasoning for smoke roast meat

> 3½ lb salt
> 8 tablespoons white sugar
> 2 tablespoons onion salt
> 4 tablespoons celery salt
> 2 tablespoons garlic salt
> 4 tablespoons paprika
> 8 tablespoons black pepper
> 8 tablespoons white pepper
> 4 tablespoons crushed dill

Steaks

Four cuts of steak are normally used for quick cooking: rump, sirloin, fillet and T-bone. The latter, as the name implies, is left on the bone, and in effect is simply a cross section cut from a piece of sirloin on the bone but with the flap or 'skirt' piece removed, as this is too tough for quick cooking.

Fillet is very tender, even when it comes from sub-standard animals, and cooks very quickly. Rump is the most solid-textured of all, and must come from a young animal if it is to cook reasonably quickly. Cooking times for sirloin or T-bone steaks fall some way between those for rump and fillet. They should be rubbed well with basic seasoning half an hour before cooking, then have oil applied immediately before being placed in the pre-heated smoke oven or on the wheelbarrow grid. Fifteen to 30 minutes is usually sufficient, depending on the cut of steak.

Spareribs

Spareribs should first be cold smoked for 12 hours before cooking. Bacon spareribs are already salted and cured, but pork spareribs should be soaked in 80% brine for 30 minutes, air dried for 12 hours, then smoked. Alternatively, they can be well rubbed with basic seasoning instead of being brined. A large batch of spareribs can be cold smoked and deep frozen for future use. The spareribs should be smoke roast at 250° F until crisp, and should be turned occasionally.

Hamburgers

Equal quantities of good quality beef and pork should be minced and bound with egg yolk and basic seasoning to form cakes. These should be placed on a wire rack, with a dripping tin underneath, in a smoke oven pre-heated to 200 - 225° F. There should be plenty of dense smoke as the hamburgers will only be in the oven for about 30 minutes. They can either be left in the same position for the whole process, or can be turned halfway through.

Cured beef

Good quality lean beef should be used. Topside or leg steak is ideal, being solid-textured but flavoursome. The beef should be cured in sweet pickle at 35° F. For pieces about 2 lb cure for 3 - 5 days. Cuts of 7 - 8 lb will require 10 - 14 days in the pickle. Before pickling it is essential that the beef should have been dead for a minimum of 7 days, otherwise the fibres will not absorb the pickle properly. After curing, the meat should be washed in cold water and left to dry under refrigeration for 24 hours. Rub well with basic seasoning.

The beef will now require cold smoking for a period of 12 - 24 hours at a temperature of from 75 - 85° F, then the process should be completed in the smoke oven, pre-heated and maintained at 200° F, certainly no higher than 225° F. Close-textured beef such as topside and leg steak requires slow cooking for the best results. Cooking times will vary from 2 to 4 hours depending on the size of the cut.

Beef processed as described has a shelf life under ordinary refrigeration of at least a month and can easily be deep frozen for much longer periods. If this is done, the beef should first be cut up into suitably sized pieces, so that it can later be used as required.

Biltong

Real biltong, as produced in South Africa, consists of narrow strips of meat, salted and sun dried. The flesh of game animals is used, also ostrich, and the most highly esteemed and expensive is springbok biltong. Britain does not have a climate which is consistently dry enough and sunny enough to allow for the production of biltong by traditional methods, but it is possible to produce an excellent smoked substitute. Good cuts of beef or venison should be used, and I imagine goat's flesh would be ideal, being closely related to the antelope family. I have tried the flank and rib flesh of fallow deer, but, though the flavour was good, the flesh was too fibrous to swallow.

All fat should be trimmed off, as although the finished product will keep for a long time without refrigeration, fat will turn rancid. The meat should be cut into strips 1 - 1½ in. thick. The strips of meat are now cured in sweet pickle brine for 5 - 7 days. The meat is rinsed in fresh water and dried under refrigeration for 24 hours. The strips of meat are next cut into very thin slices with a very sharp knife. This will be easier if the meat is placed in a deep freeze until partly frozen — this will make it much firmer during slicing. Cured meat seasoning should be applied to both sides of the slices as an additional flavouring only, as the period the meat has remained in the brine will have been enough to cure it.

The meat slices can have pieces of string passed through holes made in their ends, for hanging in the smoker, or can be laid flat on racks. Cold smoking takes place at a temperature between 50°F and 85°F — actually the lower the better. According to smoke temperature and atmospheric humidity, smoking time can vary between 24 hours and 4 days. When a slice will snap in two when it is bent, the meat is ready.

There is no need to freeze the finished product, which will keep almost indefinitely when kept in a container with perforated sides or lid to allow for the free circulation of air.

Smoked rabbit pie

For this rather unusual dish you will require:
> Shortcrust pastry
> 1 full-sized rabbit
> 12 oz belly pork
> 4 eggs (smoked — see p. 66)
> 8 oz mushrooms
> 2 medium-sized onions

Ideally, the rabbit should have been dead just 3 days, and have hung at normal room temperature or been kept in a refrigerator in hot weather. After skinning, the rabbit should be well washed and allowed to soak in salt water for 3 hours. Then it should be pricked with a fork in the thickest parts of the flesh. The carcase, along with the belly pork, should be placed in 90% brine.

Rabbit and belly pork should be cold smoked for 24 hours at 75 - 90°F and should not be pre-dried before smoking commences. The rabbit is then cut into joints and placed in a casserole along with the sliced belly pork and the peeled and sliced onions. The mushrooms are now added, the contents of the casserole just covered with water, and salt and pepper sprinkled over the surface. The casserole is placed in the oven for 1½ - 3 hours, according to the age of the rabbit, at a temperature of 350°F. Alternatively, the meat, mushrooms and onions can be cooked in a pressure cooked until tender. The meat should be allowed to cool just enough so that the flesh can be removed from the bones. The rabbit meat, belly pork, mushrooms and onions are now placed in a pie dish and the smoked eggs, cut into pieces. The dish is covered with a sheet of shortcrust pastry in which a few holes are made to allow steam to escape. The pie is baked at 425°F for 20 minutes. It is equally good eaten hot or cold.

11

Storage of smoked food

I have already remarked that, owing to modern refrigeration techniques, it is no longer necessary to smoke food as a means of preservation. Many smoked foods will keep at least 3 weeks under ordinary refrigeration, and most will retain their quality for some months when deep frozen, if protected adequately against 'freezer burn'. Ordinary polythene wrapping offers no such protection but aluminium foil does and, oddly enough, so does brown paper. When food is wrapped in aluminium baking foil, the foil should be squeezed around the object so that it becomes moulded to fit the contours of the food which is to be frozen. Offering better protection still is a heavy duty opaque polythene wrapping which is used in conjunction with a vacuum packing technique in modern poultry producing establishments. The majority of such establishments will, at a small cost, vacuum pack smoked fowl, from quail to turkeys and various smoked meats, from the home smoker.

Frozen smoked food thaws out fairly rapidly. Deep freezing turns to ice the fluid content which is trapped in the tissues of the fish, flesh or fowl. The more ice that is formed, the longer it will take for the food to thaw out again. Smoking removes a good deal of this moisture, and so the smoked article thaws out quicker than the raw material.

12

Commercial production

The home smoker and his or her family will have greatly enjoyed the results of their excursions into this fascinating art.
So have their friends who have pronounced their smoked
salmon, trout and eels to be vastly superior to anything they
have tasted in the most exclusive restaurants. The rarer
delicacies they will have tasted for the first time and have no
doubt expressed amazement that such fine fare is not readily
available in better-class delicatessens.

Small wonder, then, that the home smoker may be en-
couraged to consider smoking on a grander scale, but you
would be well advised to consider certain factors before
embarking on any large-scale ventures.

Certain smoked foods are traditional and are widely accepted. Smoked salmon, trout, kippers, finnans, cod and haddock
fillets and Arbroath smokies are all well known in Britain and
the demand for these commodities is steady. Several large-
scale processing plants are already in operation and seem to
work quite profitably. This, however, makes the production
of these particular foods highly competitive and the expanding
home smoker might well find it difficult to compete with the
larger concerns, pricewise. Your products might be considerably superior to the larger company's, dependent as it is on
paid (and frequently disinterested) labour and more, hurried
processes in the interests of economy, but you will not be able

to use the vast quantities of raw material which the larger company is able to process, so you are unlikely to be able to buy at the same favourable rate and consequently will be unable to sell your finished products as cheaply as the established large concern.

What, then, of your specialities, which you alone produce and your larger rivals have probably never even heard of? What of your venison, quail, ducks, pheasants and cold smoked fillet steaks? The British as a race are notoriously conservative in their eating habits and in particular over new smoked foods. Non-shooting people in Scandinavia and Germany appear to have a far greater appreciation of venison and game, both smoked and fresh, than do their counterparts in Britain. Shooting people and game fishermen in Britain appear to be open-minded and adventurous when it comes to trying new smoked foods, but these people constitute only a small proportion of the British public. In America the situation is far different. A far larger cross section of the community are 'hunters' and fishermen, and a similar situation obtains in Scandinavia.

The home smoker is therefore largely dependent upon the great British public to buy his wares, and I am convinced that the great British public is not ready for them just yet. Another difficulty is lack of continuity. Smoked delicacies can never be cheap, if the producer is to make a decent profit, so it is quite common for a customer to make a purchase, be absolutely delighted with it, but to feel he cannot afford it again for some considerable time. Doubtless he tells his friends who say: 'Marvellous, we must try some', then promptly proceed to forget all about it.

I know that several small smoking concerns have come into being, quickly gained a good reputation, then faded out through lack of patronage. It is, therefore, my advice to any home smoker not to attempt 'go commercial' exclusively. If you can do some commercial smoking as a sideline, well and good. It will prove a profitable extension to a fascinating hobby and should slowly help to educate the public into trying and enjoying some of the rarer specialities.

If you live in a rural area, help can be obtained under a CoSIRA (Council for Small Industries in Rural Areas) scheme.

Twenty per cent of the cost of new equipment can be obtained, and an allowance for the conversion of existing buildings up to the sum of £1,000 is also available. Additional information may be obtained from your local council or Citizens' advice bureau.

Of course a licence for the production of food for sale must be obtained from the local council, but will present no problem if the grant-aided scheme is utilized and the premises brought up to the required standard. So I would encourage any home smoker to 'have a go' part-time, but would do my utmost to discourage him from burning his boats and attempting to make a full-time living from this type of work.

Appendices

1

SUMMARY OF SMOKING DO'S AND DONT'S

1 Change brine regularly and keep brining tubs clean.
2 Only use top-quality fresh fish.
3 Always remove blood channel in fish.
4 Always remove the kidney from eels.
5 Do not hang winged game for more than 3 days before brining.
6 Beef and venison must age a minimum of 1 week before brining.
7 Do not use wet fuels for smoking. It can give a mouldy flavour to the product and will hinder drying. If only wet sawdust is available, it should be thinly spread on a clean floor to dry.
8 Do not use resinous woods or a bitter flavour will be given to the product.
9 Do not leave ducklings in cold smoke for more than 36 hours or they may turn rancid.
10 When hot smoking fish, never allow smoke temperature to exceed 190° F or the fish will disintegrate. Try to keep it at 180° F.
11 Leave all products in brine for the full specified time.
12 Maintain fish at a chill temperature (32° F) while awaiting processing.
13 Use only good-quality solid salt with no magnesium additives.

14   Hang fish to dry after brining for specified times to allow to develop a good surface salt gloss.
15   Maintain smoking units and racks in clean condition.
16   Do not allow ash to accumulate.
17   Smoking should be carried out for full recommended times, at correct temperatures.
18   Always allow the product to cool completely before either packaging or deep freezing.
19   Do not eat any smoked product until it has aged at least 24 hours. If eaten before 24 hours, no harm will result but full flavour will not have developed.
20   Do not smoke very young pheasants.
21   Remember to 'feed' the cut surface of frozen salmon with oil before placing in smoker.
22   Do not smoke young grouse — they are better roasted.
23   Salmon under 8 lb should be split rather than filleted.
24   Do not over-cook venison, particularly red.
25   Always ensure that salmon loses 17% of its weight during smoking.
26   Do not let your ducks get on fire.
27   When brining poultry and winged game, make certain the body cavity of the bird is completely filled with brine.
28   If gas flame should blow out during hot smoking, remove hot smoker from gas ring in the case of a bin or barrel smoker. If a cabinet smoker is involved, give plenty of time for escaped gas to clear, as, if the gas ring is relit too soon, gas which has lodged will explode, possibly burning you and the product.
29   Solid fuels, such as small logs, can be used for smoke production, but the fire needs attention. It has to be regularly replenished and care must be taken that it does not blaze up and exceed the desired temperatures, in which case damping down with sand may be necessary. Sawdust, on the other hand, burns with a steady heat at low temperatures, and requires little attention.

2

BRINE STRENGTHS AT 60°F

	Salt per gallon of water	
	lb	*oz*
10%		4½
20%		9
30%		13¾
40%	1	3
50%	1	8½
55%	1	11
60%	1	14
65%	2	1
70%	2	4¼
75%	2	7½
80%	2	10¾
85%	2	14¼
90%	3	1¾
95%	3	5½
100%	3	9½

3

STORAGE LIFE OF CERTAIN SPECIES OF SMOKED FISH

Species	Smoked product	60°F In top condition Days	60°F Edible Days	32°F In top condition Days	32°F Edible Days
Haddock	Finnans	2-3	4-6	4-6	8-10
	Finnans (straws)	1-2	2½-3	4	6-7
	Smokies (hot smoked)	1-2	2½-3	3-4	5-6
Herring	Kippers	2-3	5-6	4-6	10-14
	Buckling (hot smoked)	1-2	2-3	3-4	5-6
Salmon	Fillets and split fish (cold smoked)	3-4	5-6	5	11
Trout	Whole (hot smoked)	3	7	6	10

Some of the keeping times given may not seem very long for well cured products, but allow for a good margin of safety healthwise.

4

STORAGE LIFE OF GENERAL TYPES OF SMOKED FISH IN DEEP FREEZE CONDITIONS

	Type of fish	
	*Smoked white fish**	*Smoked fatty fish***
At 15°F		
Good	1 month	3 weeks
Inedible	3 months	2 months
At −5°F		
Good	3½ months	2 months
Inedible	10 months	5 months
At −29°F		
Good	7 months	Over 1 year
Inedible	4½ months	Over 9 months

*Finnans, cod and haddock fillets
**Salmon, mackerel, kippers, eels, buckling

5

RELATIVE HUMIDITY OF THE ATMOSPHERE IN RELATION TO SMOKE CURING

Notes on measurement

Two ordinary mercury-in-glass thermometers are required with a range of about 50-100° F. They must be inserted through holes in the wall of the kiln a few inches apart so that the bulbs project well into the smoke stream. One of the thermometers (the 'wet bulb') has a muslin bag or sleeve tied round the bottom inch or two of the stem, so that it completely surrounds the mercury bulb.

Before a reading is taken, this bag is moistened by dipping in clean water, preferably distilled water, and after putting back in position, the reading of the thermometer is taken when it is steady after about half a minute. The ordinary temperature of the dry bulb should be read on the other thermometer at the same time as that of the wet bulb. The smoke should not pass over the wet bulb immediately before the dry bulb in case the air gets cooled by evaporation before affecting the dry bulb.

From the two readings, the relative humidity of the air or smoke expressed in percentage of saturation with moisture vapour at the dry bulb temperature is obtained using the table of figures given above.

The temperature of the wet bulb is normally lower than that of the dry bulb, because, as the water on the muslin

Percentage relative humidities of air from readings of temperatures of wet and dry bulb thermometers

Dry bulb, °F	Difference between dry and wet bulb temperatures, °F																			
	1	2	3	4	5	6	7	8	9	10	11	12	13	14	15	16	17	18	19	20
70	95	90	86	81	77	72	68	64	59	55	51	48	44	40	36	33	29	25	22	19
71	95	90	86	81	77	72	68	64	60	56	52	48	45	41	37	33	30	27	23	20
72	95	91	86	82	77	73	69	65	61	57	53	49	45	42	38	34	31	28	24	21
74	95	91	86	82	78	74	69	65	61	58	54	50	47	43	39	36	33	29	26	23
75	96	91	86	82	78	74	70	66	62	58	54	51	47	44	40	37	34	30	27	24
76	96	91	87	82	78	74	70	66	62	59	55	51	48	44	41	38	34	31	28	25
77	96	91	87	83	79	74	71	67	63	59	56	52	48	45	42	39	35	32	29	26
78	96	91	87	83	79	75	71	67	63	60	56	53	49	46	43	39	36	33	30	27
79	96	91	87	83	79	75	71	68	64	60	57	53	50	46	43	40	37	34	31	28
80	96	91	87	83	79	75	72	68	64	61	57	54	50	47	44	41	38	35	32	29
81	96	92	88	84	80	76	72	68	65	61	58	55	51	48	45	42	39	36	33	30
82	96	92	88	84	80	76	72	69	65	61	58	55	51	48	45	42	39	36	33	30
83	96	92	88	84	80	76	73	69	66	62	59	56	52	49	46	43	40	37	34	32
84	96	92	88	84	80	76	73	69	66	62	59	56	52	49	46	43	40	37	35	32
85	96	92	88	84	80	77	73	70	66	63	60	57	53	50	47	44	41	39	36	33
86	96	92	88	84	81	77	73	70	66	63	60	57	53	50	47	44	42	39	36	33
87	96	93	88	85	81	77	74	70	67	64	61	57	54	51	48	46	43	40	37	34
88	96	92	88	85	81	77	74	70	67	64	61	57	54	51	48	46	43	40	37	35
89	96	92	89	85	81	78	74	71	68	65	61	58	55	52	49	47	44	41	39	36
95	96	93	89	86	82	79	76	73	69	66	63	61	58	55	52	49	47	44	42	39
96	96	93	89	86	82	79	76	73	69	66	63	61	58	55	52	50	47	44	42	39
97	96	93	89	86	83	79	76	73	70	67	64	61	58	56	53	50	48	45	43	40
98	96	93	89	86	83	79	76	73	70	67	64	61	58	56	53	50	48	45	43	40
99	96	93	89	86	83	80	77	73	70	67	64	62	59	56	54	51	49	46	44	41
100	96	93	89	86	83	80	77	73	70	68	65	62	59	56	54	51	49	46	44	41

sleeve dries, it cools the mercury bulb and lowers the temperature read on the scale. The drier the air, the greater the 'wet bulb depression', ie the dry bulb temperature *minus* the wet bulb temperature.

If the air is completely saturated with moisture vapour, ie

the relative humidity is 100%, no further evaporation can take place, the wet sleeve cannot dry and thus the wet bulb reading is the same as that of the dry bulb.

While the flavours are mostly due to the smoke and the initial salting treatments, the flesh texture is largely dependent on the drying process. The amount of drying to which the product has been subjected before smoking will, of course, also affect the final product texture.

Efficient drying processes depend on the humidity of the surrounding atmosphere. The degree of saturation of the air with water vapour is termed the relative humidity (RH). Air which is completely saturated is at 100% RH, and air containing half as much water vapour as it can hold at any temperature is said to be at 50% RH. The best range of relative humidity for cold smoking purposes, where temperatures of 85° F are used, is between 60 and 70%. Where RH is above 70% the drying process is too slow, and if below 60% the fish surface dries too quickly.

In other words, the air and smoke draught speed and their capacity to dry products depends on how much the air entering the smoke unit is warmed by the fire. Where cool, dry air enters and is warmed, it will be much lighter than the air outside and will thus travel rapidly up the smoke unit and over the product. The quantity of water vapour which this air will absorb depends on its temperatures, so that if the cool dry air is warmed on entering the smoke unit, its drying capacity will be considerably increased. Where humid ambient conditions exist, the already warm, saturated air cannot be further warmed quickly enough to reduce the water vapour content and thus its capacity for drying the product is reduced.

Thus in the first stage of any smoking process moisture is removed at a rate dependent on the drying capacity of the air and smoke and their speed over the product. During the second stage of the process, when the surface has dried somewhat, its temperature gets closer to that of the air and smoke. The rate of drying becomes slower, however, as moisture has now got to move out from the inner layers of the flesh. If the initial drying stage is carried out at too high a temperature, too quickly, the result will be to harden the fish surface, making it difficult to remove inner moisture. In this instance there may be no drying effect at the centre of the product.

In hot smoking, the product must not at first be subjected to the higher temperatures involved. The process should start at a relatively low temperature to enable the product to dry partially and the skin to harden. Only then should the heat be increased to cook and smoke the product. Where too high a temperature is reached in the early stage of the process, the product cooks quickly, and as it is still soft and moist, it will break and fall into the fire.

When smoking fatty fish, the initial drying period can be reduced, using a slightly higher temperature, as the presence of some oil prevents hardening of the surface. However, the oil also retards the movement of moisture from below the flesh surface and thus the overall time of the drying process becomes longer.

As spoilage bacteria are more active in moisture-laden products, the drying process is very important. The keeping time of the product will depend, to a large extent, on the amount of moisture removed. Products which have been lightly smoke cured will spoil almost as fast as the raw material from which they were made. Products which have been very heavily cured may keep for many months at normal temperature.

Food will, of course, lose weight during the drying process as the water content is evaporated, and cold smoke cures with a weight loss of 12-18% on drying will result in good-quality products. Cooked products, obtained when hot smoked, will generally lose considerably more weight than this. The length of the drying process will depend, to a great extent, on the experience of the smoker regarding a particular smoke cure, and will involve consideration of such factors as flesh texture, prevailing weather conditions and whether cold or hot smoking is involved.

6

METRIC AND IMPERIAL CONVERSION TABLES

Capacity

1 gallon	=	4.55 litres
1 litre	=	0.22 gallon
1 pint	=	0.57 litre
1 litre	=	1.76 pints

Weight

1 lb	=	0.45 kg
1 kg	=	2.20 lb
1 oz	=	28.35 g
10 g	=	0.35 oz

Temperature

To convert Fahrenheit to Centigrade: subtract 32, then multiply by 5/9.

To convert Centigrade to Fahrenheit: multiply by 5/9, then add 32.